:epahead

Writing Bids and Funding Applications

Jane Dorner is an experienced author, web designer, editor, and speaker. She has published twenty books, as sole and co-author, and has written extensively for the media and for scholarly journals on a wide variety of subjects. Her recent publications include *The Internet: A Writer's Guide* (A & C Black, 2001), *One Step Ahead: Writing for the Internet* (OUP, 2002), and *Creative Web Writing* (A & C Black, 2002).

One Step Ahead . . .

The *One Step Ahead* series is for all those who want and need to communicate more effectively in a range of real-life situations. Each title provides up-to-date practical guidance, tips, and the language tools to enhance your writing and speaking.

Series Editor: John Seely

Titles in the series

Acknowledgements

My thanks to Randall McMullan for giving me some insights in government practice, to Howard Truelove for ideas on fundraising, and to Jane Field for sharing her chapter on 'Developing and Writing Proposals for European Funding' from *Promoting European Dimensions in Lifelong Learning*, edited by John Field (The National Institute of Adult Continuing Education, 2002). All sources are quoted in the text and permission has been given to use or adapt material.

Particular thanks to Beatrice Baumgartner-Cohen for drawing cartoons that enhance the text.

Writing Bids and Funding Applications

Jane Dorner

Cartoons by Beatrice Baumgartner-Cohen

OXFORD

UNIVERSITY PRESS

OXFORD UNIVERSITY PRESS

Great Clarendon Street, Oxford OX2 6DP

Oxford University Press is a department of the University of Oxford.
It furthers the University's objective of excellence in research, scholarship,
and education by publishing worldwide in
Oxford New York
Auckland Bangkok Buenos Aires Cape Town Chennai
Dar es Salaam Delhi Hong Kong Istanbul Karachi Kolkata
Kuala Lumpur Madrid Melbourne Mexico City Mumbai Nairobi
São Paulo Shanghai Taipei Tokyo Toronto

Oxford is a registered trade mark of Oxford University Press
in the UK and in certain other countries

Published in the United States
by Oxford University Press Inc., New York

© Jane Dorner 2004

British Library Cataloguing in Publication Data
Data available

Library of Congress Cataloging in Publication Data
Data available

ISBN 0-19-860675-3

10 9 8 7 6 5 4 3 2 1

Typeset by Footnote Graphics Ltd, Warminster, Wiltshire
Printed by Ashford Colour Press, Hampshire

Contents

Introduction

What you want

The first question you will be asking is 'What have bids, proposals, and funding applications got in common?' See what varied aims all the characters in the drawing below have—and I expect you picked up this book because you have something quite different in mind yourself.

All are seeking backing, funding, work, sponsorship, patronage, aid, career advancement, expanding horizons, financial gain—whatever you like to call it. And the aim is to make the best written presentation of yourself, and sell what you do. That is the common theme of this book. The same thought-processes underlie all these written applications. And the principles of persuasive writing are the same.

The terms in this book

So what do the words in the book's title mean for you?
Consider the difference between the words in the box:

bid	an offer to do (work) at a stated price
proposal	the putting forward of something for acceptance, an offer
application	request or petition to a person or body
quotation	the amount stated for any commodity for sale
tender	an offer to supply goods at a stated fixed price
pitch	form of words used when trying to persuade someone to buy or accept something
offer	the act of offering a price or equivalent for something, a bid
submission	the act of submitting a matter to a person for decision or consideration
request	the act of asking for something; a petition; a written document of this nature

We cannot use these words interchangeably because they all
have slightly different meanings, though, as you can see, some
are very close to each other.

A bid

When you make a bid, you 'have a try' at getting or winning
something in response to a request. This may come from a
person or a public or private body or trust. They have money or a
contract for a job to award, and are inviting people to tender for
it. Your task is to offer a price together with a campaign to show
what you will do, and how you will do it. You expect to give a
written response to an identified, and clearly defined, need.

page spreads in this book that particularly apply to you ⟶ 14, 28, 31, 44, 63, 79, 84, 105, 115, 125

A proposal

When you make a proposal, you are also offering a plan of
action towards some desired outcomes. In fact, a written
proposal often forms part of your reaction to a bid. Frequently,
though, a proposal is pro-active. You want to offer the work you
do to other people and persuade them that they need you to do
it. Or you see a need for something in the workplace and make

Will you marry me?

is a standard verbal proposal.

a proposal to your line manager for a change or improvement. Perhaps you want to propose a series of social events or a festival to your local community centre. Maybe you could win a design contract if you put an appealing proposal to local companies.

14, 25, 28, 31, 33, 40, 44, 60, 63, 78, 84, 104, 106, 109 ←——— *page spreads in this book that particularly apply to you*

A funding application

If you need money to get a project off the ground, you are probably making a request for sponsorship. You will also need to write a proposal to the funder to show why they should be interested in you. In some cases, this will be a full-blown application package tailor-made to a particular funder. In others, it will be a single direct mailing letter—the same basic text sent to a large number of carefully targeted people.

15, 21, 25, 27, 48, 60, 62, 78, 94, 97, 107, 111, 119, 122, 128 ←——— *page spreads in this book that particularly apply to you*

These distinctions are rough and ready, though, because, as this book will show, the edges between all three sometimes blur into each other. Our interest here will mainly be in the general principles that unify them all. You could think of that as the dark green area in the diagram below:

Remember
Funders such as:

- banks
- venture capitalists
- business angels
- government
- charities
- trusts
- foundations

look for a 'win-win' partnership with you.

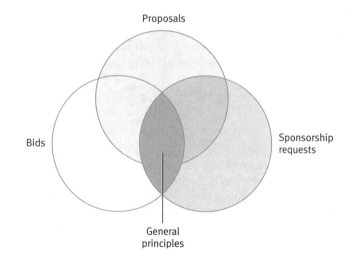

Proposals

Bids

Sponsorship requests

General principles

8

How this book will help

At the heart of a bid, proposal, or funding application is a request for financing. It may be needed for personal gain, on behalf of a group, for charity, or simply in order to develop an interesting or personally important idea or invention. Nevertheless, money is what oils the wheels of almost any project.

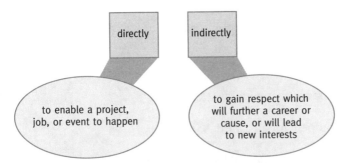

directly — to enable a project, job, or event to happen

indirectly — to gain respect which will further a career or cause, or will lead to new interests

There isn't a foolproof recipe for getting money—what works for one organization may not work for another—but this book will identify the successful ingredients.

Chapters 4 and 5 get down to the nitty-gritty of writing the application package.

It starts with the background thinking, then considers the negotiating phases, and looks at the preparation of a campaign (chapters 1 to 3). Chapters 4 and 5 take apart all the elements of the application package and the details of how to write it. Then we'll look at teams and partnerships (chapters 6 and 7).

Part B is a compendium of useful sample documents and checklists, guidelines and templates, and sources of further advice (complete with names and addresses of some key organizations). These checklists and forms are useful as *aides memoire* in the writing of bids, proposals, and funding applications. You *can* use them as props, but they make more sense if you read the explanations and occasional case histories in Part A first.

Most of the book will be directed at individuals, agencies, and institutions who need to make private, small-scale, or joint pitches.

The most likely projects fall within these broad areas, and aim to:

- offer freelance services;

- get a grant to buy time or equipment for a project;

- obtain modest sponsorship for a personal, not-for-profit, or community event;

- sell an idea to a manager, client, or board of directors;

- answer a public tender;

- propose changes at work;

- compete for an award.

Even if your situation does not exactly match any of the above, the principles of how to pitch are very similar, and it is upon those that this book will concentrate. You'll notice that words above such as 'sell', 'obtain', and 'compete' are pro-active verbs that 'push' an idea at a prospective consumer. The recipient may or may not expect this push: your offer could come out of the blue or it might be a reply to a request. The pattern usually looks like this:

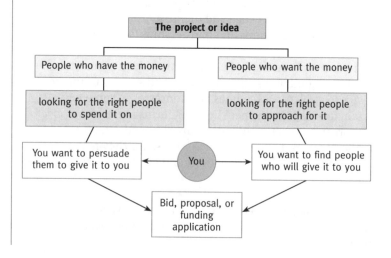

Of course, the advice to an individual looking for donations to a private event is not identical to that for a project manager piecing together an international bid. Nevertheless, the differences are mainly in the detail.

Detail of other projects is useful to make you reflect on how it applies in your own case. Sometimes it is easier to distance yourself from your own concerns, and extrapolate from other examples. So I will be giving concrete examples in different activity areas. Take from them what applies to your case.

For those who want to skip, follow the margin icons, which will show if there is a particular focus for a double-page spread (there are no margin icons where the text applies to all three activities).

 a bid

 a proposal

 a funding application

Though the detail will be different, the thinking processes all require:

- an examination of all choices and implications;

- an expression of opinion;

- persuading someone to take a course of action;

- financial calculations.

So let's get started.

1 Creative thinking

Introduction

This is the brainstorming chapter in which we'll talk about expectations—your own and the people you are approaching. Then we'll consider what sources of money might best match your requirements. And we'll touch briefly on some of the main points of any approach. These will all be expanded in later chapters.

Identify with others

Before anything else: put yourself in the other person's shoes—the person you are writing to. Everything in this book will return to this one fundamental requirement of any bid, proposal, or funding application.

Consider how you react when a door-to-door salesman arrives on your front step. It interrupts what you were doing before. Maybe you aren't in the mood for buying dusters and ironing board covers, for leukaemia donations or monthly standing orders to victims of torture. Perhaps you have developed a personal policy—you give to certain causes, but not to others; you give if it's raining; you never buy dusters; you give if you warm to the person who is trying to get your attention.

I'm willing to bet that at least once in your life, you were swayed by the right person at the right time. They empathized with you, and you responded to them. They put themselves in your shoes. You bought or gave, and both of you went away feeling good.

When making a proposal, it is important to put yourself in the other person's shoes.

The obverse of that is the sales pitch that builds on guilt; the pedlar who says: 'Oh please at least look at my wares. I'm just trying to earn an honest crust, and no one has let me open my bag all day.' Not very inviting. Why should *you* look? Trying to involve you in their problems just makes you feel bad. If you do fall for a tea-cloth, you probably feel cross and vow to be tougher next time. They haven't put themselves in your shoes.

Inconceivable as it may sometimes seem to you, the person or public body at the other end of a bid, proposal, or funding application is not hanging on your every word. Your idea may land on their desk when they are in the middle of something else (as you were when the front door-bell rang) or it may arrive because they have invited it.

Either way, it is your job to convince them that you are the right person at the right time.

The rest of this book will be looking at many different ways of doing that. In all cases, however complex the approach, it is vital to identify with the person or body you are approaching.

Who to apply to

Now that you have identified with whoever will be on the receiving end of your own pitch, the next task is to identify what sort of an organization is the right one for you. In the case of a bid or a proposal for work, your own area of expertise will determine that. If you are looking for funding, you will need to narrow down the possible sources.

It helps to have a clear understanding of the difference between various sources of money or power and the terminology currently in use. This book is mainly about getting new work, grants, and sponsorship, but there may be other equally effective ways of getting what you want. Remember that in all cases listed below, there are tax implications and you should consider those as part of your pitch. It is vital to think about all these sources of money before you start to plan and write because your approach will be different in each case.

Some tax considerations are in Part B, page 116.

Clients

Many bids or proposals are pitches for work from people who need what you or your agency can do (advertising, web site design, software solutions, window-cleaning, accountancy, and many more). Your starting point is to think how you persuade others that you offer value.

For simplicity's sake, I will be calling the person you are proposing to 'the client' though it's not always the best term. The general principles remain the same: you are in effect using the age-old proposal, 'I am a good prospect; will you marry me?'

Grants and awards

If you are seeking modest grants, you will probably start with government, charities, trusts, and foundations. Generally, they are not looking for something in return (as businesses are) but they do want to back a well-thought-out or worthy project.

The government has a wide-ranging programme of grants. The largest grants of money come from public institutions and may be awarded by government or non-governmental agencies. Some are fixed subsidies and others are given according to merit. A call for papers or proposals, or an invitation to tender will appear in the appropriate forum (newspapers, web sites, and so on). Some grants are available at any time; others have a cut-off date. Most have rigorous expectations with application guidelines.

There is also an impressive range of Trusts and Foundations covering almost every field of human endeavour. It is always worth hunting out some of the more obscure ones for which you qualify. A good starting place is to approach your local Council and enquire what voluntary sector advice they offer. Some have officers who will spend a couple of hours with you discussing your options. Many will take you through the 'Apply Yourselves' software (listed in Part B, page 119).

There is an impressive range of Trusts and Foundations covering almost every field of human endeavour.

Donations

These are gifts, usually of small sums. The donor expects a 'thank you' and may want some form of credit—though many are happy to give anonymously. This is charity-giving and may qualify for Gift Aid, which means the recipient can reclaim tax already paid by the donor.

These are the four main ways business might be able to help you:

1 Making financial contributions;
2 Sharing business expertise;
3 Providing staff volunteers;
4 Offering in-kind support.

Prize draws, auction of promises, and galas

Incentives offer useful techniques for getting money from individuals. It's still charity, but the trigger to give is the desire to win the raffle or get a bargain at an auction (where individuals offer their own expertise in exchange for a sum of money going to the cause), or attend a prestige event. These are most effective in community fundraising.

Legacies

It is not easy to sell yourself as a potential beneficiary of someone's will, but it does happen. You might be able to offer a series of benefits in exchange for a legacy commitment. A starting point for this might be the Legacy Promotion Campaign (details in Part B, page 121) which seeks to increase tax-efficient legacy giving.

Sponsorship

This is a commercial relationship where sponsor and applicant expect or deliver value for money. Sponsoring companies see this as part of their sales strategy because it can deliver tangible and intangible benefits while also exhibiting a social conscience. In particular, it aims for:

- specific results that show success;

- a payback to the community;

- positive association between the donor and the activity;

- success on a small budget;

- relationship-building between products and communities or causes.

Payment in kind

Some companies are more willing to give their product than actual cash. This is a useful form of product placement, and is widely used by young film-makers, schools, and others. A

To act from pure benevolence is not possible for finite beings. Human benevolence is mingled with vanity, interest or some other motive.

Dr Johnson

school wishing to create a nature area, for example, may find it easier to get a pond-liner from a local merchant or plants from the nearby nursery than cash to the same value.

Other possibilities are donations of unwanted furniture, computer equipment, use of a company's premises for meetings, conferences, training days, receptions, or awards ceremonies. Some companies will be happy to give volunteer services, e.g. time with a financial adviser, a computer technician, a caterer, a marketing specialist, or other role models. This could be worth a great deal.

All these are nevertheless sponsorship, and the benefits need to be spelt out.

Look at

- What you offer
- Market knowledge
- Methodology
- Outcomes
- Timeframes

Patronage and membership schemes

There is a fine line between a donor, a patron, and a sponsor. A patron or Friend, or Corporate Member, is generally able to be slightly more altruistic than a sponsor because the need to demonstrate value for money doesn't cloud the picture. A patron will normally require some form of public acknowledgement and a range of benefits. A named brick, plaque, window, seat are among the incentives to patrons (use imagination for your own particular project to see if there's something you could do). There are often different levels in friendship schemes—these are commonly labelled Gold, Silver, and Bronze. Again, imaginative naming can attract patrons.

Income

Finally, could you or your organization fund a project out of your own income? If you could sell more seats at a function, or branded mugs and T-shirts at a local event, it might be better to concentrate energy on that rather than on fundraising. Or if you want to buy time so you can fulfil a dream, could you work overtime, or save, or do some careful budgeting rather than ask outsiders for money?

Thinking through the objectives

Although it is a good idea to have a picture of the story you are going to tell, there is no point in writing anything down until you have clearly identified the aims and significance of what you propose. It will help if you think about it under the basic headings that follow. This is the brainstorming stage and you might want to make lists and notes to help you when you start to write.

What you offer

Give the client more than they want: give what they never dreamed they could have.

Clarify what you have to give and how it will benefit the recipient. Much of your bid will demonstrate:

- what you can deliver;
- how you will achieve it;
- that you are the right person to do it.

But you must put the client first. Why should they care? The current jargon talks of sponsorship partnerships. So think of yourself as a partner, not a petitioner, and focus on what you have to give. Be careful not to be too forceful, however, because it can come across as blackmail if you are not careful and that rarely works. Ideally, you want to *show* that you offer quality or value without saying it. Show, don't tell.

Market knowledge

Do you know the market or can you acquire the knowledge you do not have? The client or funder will want to feel safe in your hands. Let's imagine you propose to create a database of endangered species to teach schoolchildren about the environment. The 'market' is the future generation who will be responsible for a well-balanced world. So make it clear what your educational qualifications are, and what angle you are approaching this from. It could be to interest a client in a saleable software product (enhanced by association with a worthy project), or it could be to attract sponsorship for a free online learning package.

Either way, effective use of detail is persuasive. You need to show that you have the right contacts, a working knowledge of environmental issues, technical understanding of the way databases operate, and so on. Show that you know the terminology that fits the subject. So, for example, your database might have fields for location, habitat, diet, lifestyle, threats, current population, and seasonal activity. It would be a mistake to overdo the detail at this early stage; just give enough to convince the client that you do know your subject.

Methodology

Think about what you are going to deliver, and how. Your proposal will outline the intended methodology, along with timings for the various different project phases. This will involve deciding which of the following you plan to do:

See also Part B, page 105, for more detail on methodology.

- show how you will do what you propose (will you use questionnaires, surveys, interviews, studies, software, etc.?);

- consider the format of the final piece (is it a written report, a presentation, a conference, an event, performance, or fulfilling a piece of work?);

- carry out a consultation or create links with local businesses or services;

- report back to the client (how and when will you do this?);

- give recommendations or performance (e.g. if you are doing a piece of research, will you be making recommendations?; or if you are asking for funding, what is the performance or event that is the culmination of all your work?);

- confirm that you have done what you propose (how are you going to show this?).

Outcomes

Clients like specific detail because everyone can then see very clearly how the final result matches up to the initial proposal. You cannot always measure benefits (social advantages, for example, are hard to quantify), but where you can, try to set down clear goals, like those on the following page.

See also the sports proposal model letter in Part B, page 107.

Interest 8 new companies in the market.

Expose the funder's brand to 12,000 possible visitors.

Attract 7 new advertisers.

Identify 10 candidates who will continue the project.

Draft a three-year programme of future work.

Be careful, as any promises made in the proposal will be evaluated later (if you are successful). It can be helpful if you are able to find some statistics in a similar field to yours to back up any claims you make. For example, you could quote a success story like this one.

The whisky supplier Glenmorangie sponsored the Glasgow Jazz Festival to pep up its flagging image among young people. After the festival it sent out an evaluation questionnaire which showed that:

■ about 11.2 million people were exposed to the product through media coverage;

■ 97% of the people surveyed thought it was good to see Glenmorangie sponsoring jazz;

■ 76% said it gave the company a more contemporary feel.

As a result, the company repositioned its brand as 'The Spirit of the Festival'.

A spirited performance.

Using imagination

Was it a stroke of imagination to get Bryant & May to sponsor the play *The Matchmaker* or was it just obvious? Sometimes an ideal partnership is staring you in the face and you do not see it. Look at your own venture and see if you can identify the perfect partner for it.

A new theatre company called '**ice**and**fire**', for example, seeking funding for its first performance, could target fridge and freezer manufacturers in the area. Is there a link to your name, group, or street name that you could exploit?

Some ideas

■ Search Debrett's (free) for people who share your birthday or your surname at <http://www.debretts.co.uk/> or look at <http://www.famousbirthdays.com/>. With a personal 'handle' perhaps you can persuade someone famous to champion your cause, either financially or by using their name.

■ Search the reference books in KnowUK <http://www.knowuk.co.uk/> looking for hobbies, interests, and clubs to identify people who might be sympathetic to your venture. For example, I once searched the online version of *Who's Who* looking for well-known people who had an interest in chess in order to find a patron for a literary festival that had chess as its theme.

■ Look for famous people of the past with whom you could find a connection and see if there is a possible lead. Try <http://amillionlives.com/>.

■ Try chronologies in your field of interest to see whether you can relate an event date to something that happened in history (type 'chronology + subject' into your favourite search engine). This could offer a hook to catch a funder with a special interest.

■ Consider inviting an individual to become a Trustee, or member of an Advisory Group or Steering Group to gain their expertise.

> **Tip**
> KnowUK is a library subscription service providing key information about the people, institutions and organizations in the UK. It brings together in a single electronic source almost all of the most authoritative reference materials in any library, including *Who's Who* and *Hansard*.

■ Hold a 'trivia' evening or a 'sale of promises', asking local shops, individuals, and industries to donate goods or services. Then auction these to the highest bidders. You could offer a prize for the item that raised the most money.

■ If you are targeting local industries, consider whether they might see sponsorship as part of a recruitment drive. For example, many requests for personal development projects come from people who have just left school, college, or university. Many industries find it useful to forge links with young people who show some entrepreneurial skills and job offers can often result.

When you have found your perfect partner, find out as much as you can about them before you begin your approach. The cautionary tale below illustrates how easily you could find yourself in an embarrassing position.

Cautionary tale

A cancer charity was approached by a leading confectionery brand. The company wanted to donate a sizeable sum of money and establish an ongoing fundraising relationship. One of the company's aims was to get some publicity from making the donation. The company has a parent company that contributed towards the donation. A cheque presentation was requested and arranged.

On the day, the charity discovered that the confectionery brand is actually owned by a major US cigarette manufacturer and their name was on the cheque.

A surprisingly large number of journalists turned up for the presentation, but it was not the kind of publicity the company wanted.

To sum up . . .

1. Think how you react to requests for work or for money as it will help you identify with people you are approaching yourself.

2. Clarify what you are asking for.

3. Pin-point the client or source of funding most appropriate for your work.

4. Demonstrate your market knowledge.

5. Make sure you have a methodology for thinking through the details from first proposal to final outcome.

6. Then work out what you offer and how you can use your imagination to sell the idea to someone else.

Ask not what your country can do for you—ask what you can do for your country.

President Kennedy, in his first inaugural address

Use your imagination to find appropriate sponsorship.

2 | Preparing the pitch

Negotiation phases

In today's world, there is a great deal of emphasis on creating a business relationship between a provider (of funds, resources, or services) and the recipient (individual, event, or organization). The 'trick' is to find a common cause in which the provider and the recipients can join forces.

It may take several negotiation phases while the two parties come to an agreement about where their mutual interests lie. This process is not necessarily linear. You may move backwards and forwards through a series of phases like the ones in the diagram. Or you may just get one chance of getting it right first time. At each stage, think where you are in the full project and how close to the summit '*', the final bid or proposal, you are. There may be several stages before you are ready to write anything down. Try to observe at which stage you are, and to where you are moving.

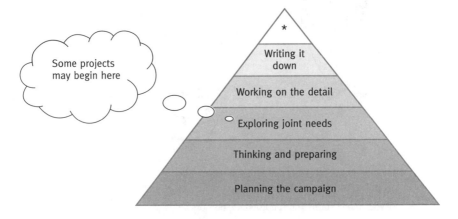

Some projects may begin here

*

Writing it down

Working on the detail

Exploring joint needs

Thinking and preparing

Planning the campaign

Targeting

Targeting relies on matching what you have to offer with what the other person is looking for. For fundraising and unsolicited proposals to clients, this will typically fall within these areas:

- Improving their image—this could be by association with a lifestyle connection that you offer.

- Making the brand popular—can you help communicate a positive message?

- Corporate hospitality—could sponsoring an event provide a client with a social occasion at a rate competitive with holding a party in a costly venue?

- Community relations—will your proposal make an impact on relationships within the community?

- Media exposure—if you expect significant publicity, then anyone sponsoring you will be exposed to it too.

- Differentiation from competition—perhaps an association with you will make the organization stand out from the crowd.

- Future prosperity—financial as well as building trust.

If you have something specific to offer in any of the above, then make a point of saying so. You also need to be aware of where a company wants to position itself. Knowing their marketing objectives will help you give the right spin to a proposal.

Here are some typical manufacturers' needs:

Beer	To attract a younger market (but also to promote responsibility in drink/driving)
Soap powder	To reinforce name awareness and image
Cars	To achieve test drives/showroom traffic
Newspapers	To increase young readership
Banks	To attract student market
Rice range	To underline ethnic authenticity
Soft drinks	To reach mothers with young children and also gain approval of schools

Consider
What can you do to match your plans with their objectives?

See page 24.

I have already suggested avoiding later embarrassment by finding out about the company you are pitching at. It is also important because the people who have asked for tenders want reassurance that you have understood them and their requirements.

"La Belle" Ltd.
Products by women for women

A pitch coming out of the blue is rarely effective.

If your pitch comes out of the blue, they will want to feel there is some personalization in the approach. A mass mailing is instantly recognizable and rarely effective. So, at the very least, top and tail a general letter with something designed to appeal to the organization or person you are writing to. Telephone beforehand to get the name of the right person in the right department.

Read the company history (get its annual report or look at its web site) and be alert to any special targeting clues. What are the Managing Director's or Chairman's special interests? Is there something in the mission statement that 'clicks' with one of your aims? Read looking for anything you can build on.

✘ *Don't write*

Dear Sir or Madam,

✘ *Don't write*

Dear PR Manager,

✔ *Do write*

Dear
[Correctly-spelled named person],

You might notice, for example, that they have a special anniversary event coming up. If so, they will be more eager to promote the company image, possibly even hang a rebadging campaign on it. If your proposal arrives on their desk when they are beginning to think about the anniversary date— say 18 months in advance—and you weave in an idea that makes your proposal fit in with their aims, you are much more likely to get a favourable hearing.

Case history

Here is an example of canny targeting. The Norfolk Rural Life Museum wanted to put on an exhibition called 'Life and Death in the Workhouse'. They wanted it to look at death from a historical perspective, but also at how death is dealt with in the present day.

Background

Exhibitions are expensive, so the museum approached a local company, Anglia Funeral Services, for funding. They told Anglia that the company name, and therefore its services, would be linked to the exhibition in a positive way.

As it happened, Anglia had just won an award for a staff development programme that made much of integration with the local community. The company wanted to build on this success. The Museum proposed a three-year educational programme to take into local schools, and Anglia saw the competitive advantage this would give them.

Link your project with business in a positive way.

Commercial logic

The collaboration between the 'Life and Death in the Workhouse' exhibition and Anglia Funeral Services is clear, and the sponsorship gave good potential for local publicity. By working with schools and making a taboo subject accessible, Anglia Funeral Services were aiming to educate people for the good of their business and the community in general— promoting their name as a family-run, community-spirited business.

From 'It worked for them' at Arts & Business [online] <http://www.aandb. org.uk/content/ projects/01pThespon. shtml> [accessed August 2003].

First approaches

Many approaches begin informally with a chance encounter and chat. This is not always possible. For fundraising letters, for example, it would not be realistic. The chances are that you will send out as many as you can, blindly hoping for a 2% take-up (about as much as you can hope for). All the same, find out as much as you can about the individual you are writing to before you start. This is where the Internet can help. Check the web site; find the name of the individual in charge—if personal details are on the site, find something to refer to so your letter connects to their interests more rapidly.

Some people carry this to extremes. I heard of an advertising agency whose company had missed the deadline for a pitch. Nevertheless, they knew the managing director was a fan of a particular football club. So they sent their bid by special courier (female) decked in the club's livery and with presentation ribbons in its colours. It got the boss's attention and they got the job. Sometimes audacity pays off—in advertising it often might. For many purposes, however, flair and flourish can easily misfire. If you send your proposal in a pink envelope with the letter on luminous yellow paper with purple ink, I'm afraid it will get short shrift. If what you do to get noticed is just an obvious attempt to stand out from the rest, then the chances are it will be the first to be binned. It must stand out because of its persuasiveness or excellence. Nothing else will do. But the little extra might tip the balance.

Cold calling

By far the most disheartening way of making an initial approach is 'cold calling'—i.e. telephoning to interest someone in an idea or dropping by unannounced. You don't know the person you are calling and they don't know you. You have a few seconds in which to interest them enough to continue to listen to you.

Freelance journalists have to propose new stories all the time. If they have a breaking story, they want to whet the editor's appetite just enough and no more. They do not write in because there may not be time: they therefore have to talk so they can let out a bit at a time until they have the editor hooked and willing to buy. Other proposals require a similar technique, especially if you want to bid for a contract that you have heard about but have not been invited to tender.

Between 10.30 and 12.30 a.m. are optimum times for this, to avoid start-of-day priorities, long lunches, press conferences, and end-of-day tiredness. It requires a special sort of confidence.

Email

Email is gradually replacing cold calling. You may expect to be ignored, but perhaps that's not as bad as the verbal brush off or the never-answered telephone messages. However, people get so much junk mail nowadays that emails from people they do not know may get deleted unread. One ploy is to make telephone contact, and say you will follow it up with an email, or vice versa.

Email is useful once you have got 'your toe in the door'. Once a dialogue starts, some of the pre-chat about a project will happen by email. It is less invasive than the phone, and some exchanges can initiate a rapport between people. You can understand a great deal about someone from the way in which they respond to emails. Follow their level of formality, remembering that flippancy only works with people you know. Get back to a client within the working day if you are serious about wanting to get the bid, proposal, or funding application accepted. However, do not expect them to respond to you within a similar time-frame. The client is likely to hold you a little at bay, to slow down the pace of exchange so that it does not become overwhelming. When you reply, keep the message short and to the point.

Email gives useful background documentation which helps as you draw up the proposal, but nothing replaces face-to-face meetings—'F2F' or 'fleshmeets' as they are now distastefully

From: Jane
To: Joe
Subject: Funding

Hello Joe,

You don't know me, but I wondered if you would like to give me £10,000. I have a really good idea, you see, and I've heard you're rich.
You can phone me at home at any time.

Cheers
Jane

called. It helps enormously if you have met the client, because it is so much easier to put yourself into someone's shoes if you have seen them.

Personal contact

Similarly, they trust you more if you have met and perhaps socialized a little. Unfortunately, only 6 to 10 out of 100 bids to public bodies get short-listed. It is only human nature to favour someone you think you can relate to. Vital as the writing is, so is a certain amount of networking at functions where people in your field gather.

There are many reasons why people do not or cannot network. Nevertheless, your aim in the first stage of a proposal is to secure a meeting. The written proposal will be only one stage of an entire project. Meetings, presentations, and follow-up discussions are almost certain to occur before the client accepts the idea, design, or proposal you are offering.

Even if the first, verbal stage of the proposal meets with approval, you will still have to lay it down formally on paper. This is because your contact:

■ cannot remember everything you said;

■ needs to discuss it with others;

■ requires more detail for further analysis;

■ prefers written confirmation for the avoidance of doubt.

Persistence pays
Be prepared to resend the initial proposal letter (indeed possibly the whole package).

Try not to put anything in the first approach that gives them an excuse to say 'no' straight away. Try not to give a fixed price at this early stage, but possibly a range from £X to £Y. The purpose of the initial proposal letter is to get a meeting. If there is no reply, follow it up with a telephone call and indicate that you can negotiate on any of your offers and requests.

The brief

Most projects, but not all, begin with a brief, or call for proposals. Even if there isn't one, because you are initiating the proposal yourself, there will often be guidelines, specifications, submission criteria, or some written materials stating what kinds of project or funding opportunities an organization is open to. For present purposes, we'll call that the brief.

If you have to invent your own, take apart the guidelines and create a checklist of your own. Use the sample guidelines in Part B, pages 104 ff.

It is often said that a bid is only as good as the brief that requested it. To some extent, this is true. If the client has not thought through their needs, then the bid cannot answer the brief. It can be part of the bidder's task to draw out and anticipate the client's requirements.

It is impossible to prepare a good bid from a poor brief.

Sometimes you'll be invited to pitch; sometimes you'll answer an open call. If you are invited, then you start with a small advantage: the client knows you or has heard something good about you. Find out who else is in the running. Then read the brief very carefully—between the lines as well—and interrogate it.

The questions you should be asking include the standard journalists' sextet:

- **What**—What exactly does the brief ask for? What will be the success criteria? What response are they expecting to see and have you got the skills? What are the critical issues you must address? What's the purpose?

- **Why**—Why have they come to you, or why are you responding?

- **When**—When is the proposal due? When can the work be done?

- **How**—How will you respond: a written proposal, a storyboard and presentation, both? How many roles are involved and can you fulfil them on your own or do you need others to help? How rigid are the specifications?

*I keep six honest serving-men
(They taught me all I knew);
Their names are What and Why and When
And How and Where and Who. I send them over land and sea, I send them east and west;
But after they have worked for me, I give them all a rest.*

Rudyard Kipling, *The Elephant's Child*

■ **Where**—Where is the finance? Where is the evidence that they've got the budget?

■ **Who**—Who are they? Who are the decision makers? Who are their competitors? Who are their customers? Who wrote the brief?

Answering these, and other, questions will help you to understand the brief and also to find out what else you need to know. Clarifying the brief with the client at an early stage saves everyone's time.

PEST analysis

One useful way of querying the brief is to divide a sheet of paper into four quarters and brainstorm each of these headings in relation to the project.

Equal opportunities
If you can stress how you will approach equal opportunities, it can count very much in your favour.

Political factors	**Economic factors**
Government legislation	National economy
Employment law	Industry sector
Health and safety	Decline or growth
Environmental	Client's finances
Equal opportunities	
Industry-specific	

Socio-cultural factors	**Technological factors**
Consumer tastes or preferences	Technological change
Pressure groups	Software or hardware needed
Recreation sector (arts, sports, etc.)	Product development

See also Role-play, page 85.

A PEST analysis shows the broader contextual issues influencing the business (Political, Economic, Socio-cultural, and Technological). There is often confusion between this and a SWOT analysis which works in the same way and looks at market dynamics (Strengths, Weaknesses, Opportunities, and Threats). Either (or both) can be useful for background thinking about a project.

Demonstrating understanding

A good proposal is one that:

- reflects the client's own expectations;
- marks you out as distinctive;
- doesn't overburden the client with too much extra reading.

Confirmation

When you have thoroughly analysed the brief (or invented your own) and thought a bit about how you will answer it, confirm your understanding of what the client wants—in writing. A successful proposal will demonstrate an interest in the client's needs. By summarizing what you have heard, you will demonstrate to the client that you have really been listening to their concerns and that you understand them.

Check details as many times as you need. It doesn't look like inefficiency; it looks like concern. But it doesn't do to repeat back, parrot-fashion, what's in the brief. You must refine your summary so it demonstrates that you understand even the things they have *not* said.

Once you've got the green light on your idea, further confirmation in writing is advisable. It is vital as an insurance against the unfortunate circumstances when a project does not go according to plan, and it is necessary to demonstrate the exact terms of what you agreed.

If there is no formal legal agreement, put in writing:

- what they have asked for;
- what you are planning to do;
- what is *not* included;
- the payment you have agreed;
- by when;
- dates when payment is due;

and make sure they confirm their agreement to your letter—in writing.

See Part B, page 118, for an example of the Terms and Conditions you might expect.

Who puts it in writing

Silly question if this is an individual application—you, of course. If you are part of a larger group, then one person will normally act as the channel between the group and the client. It is very confusing for clients to have to deal with more than one person—at least until you all get to know each other very well.

This can be a bottleneck, because it is possible that the people writing the bid are working for the person who has secured the initial contact. The client can feel they have built up a relationship of trust with that person, only to start all over again with someone new. It is useful to introduce others in the team as early as you can.

Identifying the competition

Writing a proposal is a considerable amount of work. So consider who you are up against before you decide how much time to commit to it. You can ask for information about who else is applying (and you may or may not be told) or you can make some informed guesses.

If it's a bid to a client, you will want to consider:

- whether they have worked with your competitor before;

- whether your role is to act as a foil for the people you suspect they will select anyway, or whether the approach to you is genuine;

See also page 63.

- whether they might steal your ideas and use a competitor to do the work; what safeguards have you got against that?;

- whether they are looking for a new image, rebrand, or change of direction (which often means a genuine wish to work with new people).

If it's a proposal for a grant or an award, you will want to consider:

- how many people normally apply;

- whether they can give you an idea of the success rate for someone in your position.

If it's a request for sponsorship, think about:

- what their annual sponsorship budget is and what volume of requests they get;
- when is the best time of year to apply.

To sum up...

1. Be closely attentive to the client's needs, or the funder's requirements. Unless what you want to do fits their needs like a glove, you are wasting your time.

2. Establish a relationship before you start to write a proposal even if it is only a tentative telephone introduction (not appropriate for large calls for tenders).

3. Checklist the specifications (see Part B, page 111ff.) and match the customer's or funder's criteria *in every detail*.

4. The initial proposal letter should give:
   - a rationale for a link with the client;
   - benefits to the client;
   - options for level of involvement;
   - endorsements;
   - media opportunities.

Be **SMART**

Specific—identify exactly what you propose and why.

Measurable—think how you will demonstrate you've achieved this.

Agreed—confirm everyone has the same understanding.

Realistic—show your aims are achievable and risk-assessed.

Time limited—say what will happen and when.

3 | Developing a campaign

Introduction

Chapters 1 and 2 have concentrated on the background to the project you are about to undertake, its rationale, where to go to 'sell' the idea, and coping with the initial stages of assessing a consumer's requirements.

This chapter moves forward from there, and reviews the stages of the campaign that come before writing the application (which is covered in the next chapter).

I use the word 'campaign', though for you it may be a drive for promotion, a way of offering of services, or preparation for localized fundraising. The planning phases may vary accordingly. Here is a useful route:

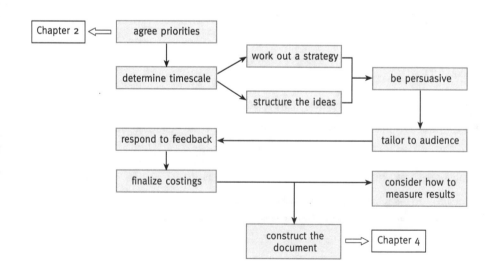

Timeframes

It's always good to plan ahead. A good rule of thumb is to allow
six months from the first approach (which may be verbal or
written) to the fruition of the idea. Of course, it depends on the
complexity, but if you have allowed less time than that, you
may have problems.

You should say when the project is starting and when it is due
to end. For complex projects, give milestones for evaluation
and payment along the way. For example, I often offer a phased
approach so that the client can choose to continue or to stop
after each phase.

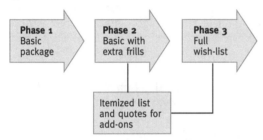

It's useful at this point to anticipate contingency arrangements
if anything goes wrong and say what you will do:

- if you are responsible;

- if the client or funder is responsible;

- if it is caused by outside forces.

See also Risk
analysis, page 96.

The plan should demonstrate that you are used to working to
deadlines, and show how you are going to chart your own
progress, and in what form.

For example, tell the client that at the end of phase 1, you will
sum up what you have done so far, bill them for the agreed
amount, and summarize the tasks to be done in phase 2. If
appropriate, supply a timeline or Gantt chart.
Timeframes are linked to finances.

See page 82 for an
example of a Gantt
chart.

See pages 46ff.

Structure

The next thing to think about is what you will say to the person on the receiving end of your proposition. Essentially, you are telling them a story. Like all good stories, it has a:

In music, the classical form is:
Exposition
Development
Recapitulation.

In science, it is:
Experiment
Method
Results.

Beginning

a statement of the current position (Once upon a time, there was . . .)

Middle

an argument or action that transmits ideas (. . . but a dragon guarded the castle so they . . .)

End

your intended outcome (. . . and they all lived happily ever after.)

Aristotle defined a story with a plot as being about the successful change from one status quo to another, to the emotional satisfaction of the audience.
In the dramas of his day, this took place within a three-act structure. This is still the basis for most plays and films today.

A bid, proposal, or funding application generally follows this basic pattern. The middle is always the longest section as it is here that the 'story' develops. If mnemonics help you refine your approach, think of it as the five **P**s:

Beginning

Preamble (the attention grabber) (P1)

Middle

Position (where we are now) (P2)
Problem or Practicalities (why we cannot stay here)
  or (what we do while we are here) (P3)
Possibilities (what else we could do) (P4)

End

Proposal (where we should go instead) (P5)

How might this work in practice in these three examples?

3 Developing a campaign

1. A proposal to redesign office spaces

P1. Why you are proposing this.

P2. What the offices are like now.

P3. Why that is unsatisfactory.

P4. A range of alternatives including moving offices.

P5. A design, campaign, and costing.

2. A bid for a large office painting contract

P1. What the client has requested.

P2. Specifications and detailed costings to achieve this.

P3. Contingencies for unexpected additions.

P4. Special terms, reductions on quantity, or negotiation on deadlines.

P5. Repetition of price, terms, and conditions.

3. Sponsorship for a mural artist

P1. How mural painting benefits the funder.

P2. How much money you want.

P3. What you can do for that.

P4. Why you are the best person.

P5. Repetition of offer with willingness to be flexible.

If you turn to the sponsorship profiling template on pages 111ff., you will see that this too is just a development of the structure presented here. Choose your own preferred structure, and make sure every bid, proposal, or funding application that you write follows an equivalent form.

A written piece—whether it is one side of A4 or an extended booklet—will need to fulfil the basic principles outlined here if it is to make itself felt.

Chapters 4 and 5 will flesh out the details.

Being persuasive

I have already talked about the importance of reading the brief or application guidelines on page 31. Part of that process involves demonstrating understanding, or common ground. We also considered the bidding structure in terms of the five **P**s (on the previous page). We could add a sixth: **P**ersuasion.

After establishing common ground (the **P**osition), you need all your powers of persuasion to move from sifting all the evidence (**P**roblem and/or **P**ossibilities) to your desired solution (**P**roposal).

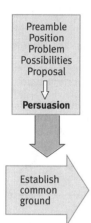

Preamble
Position
Problem
Possibilities
Proposal

⇩

Persuasion

Establish common ground → Review evidence → Compare solutions → Offer a resolution

For example

A toddler wants an ice-cream. Which approach works best, 1 or 2?

1.

'Buy me a five-flavoured ice-cream cornet *now*, or I'll shout and scream and kick all the way home.'

2.

'It's a hot day, isn't it?' *(Common ground)*

'Ooh look, an ice-cream barrow. Ice-cream cools you down, doesn't it?' *(Evidence)*

'We could look for a water fountain, but a drink isn't as nice and doesn't last as long.' 'I won't be so hot if you carry me.' 'Can I take my dress off?' *(Compare solutions)*

'If you buy me an ice-cream, we'll both be happy as it will keep me quiet and you prefer that. I really want lemon, chocolate, raspberry, pistachio, *and* vanilla, but I'll settle for any combination if that's all you can afford.' *(Resolution)*

Use your powers of persuasion to achieve your desired solution.

Most people are so close to their particular cause that they do not sufficiently think about how it comes across to someone outside it. People do often behave in self-obsessed ways (like our toddler). Sometimes, they are so bound up in their own project that they forget to put their own names on the documentation. Believe me; this is so. Applicants assume the reader will know who they are because they cannot imagine anything else.

You need imagination. Remember that your aim is to request something or influence the recipient to act in a certain way.

Another enemy to persuasion is over-enthusiasm. It is common for people, close to their own subject, to want to include everything that is relevant and clutter the final document with excess material. This does not help your cause. Readers don't want 'nice-to-know' information. They want you to be selective on their behalf.

Knowing your audience

Persuasive writing, in any field, is dependent on knowing who your audience is and how to address it. The standard advice for any journalist or features writer pitching for work is to buy several issues of the magazine in question, and study the content and style. The content will show you what sells to that readership; the style shows you how to write the article (and how to address the Editor). It is quite simply a waste of time proposing an article on 'Sugar Sculpture' to *Cosmopolitan*, which has a bent towards sex and life-style. You could propose it to *Good Housekeeping* (with a focus on table decoration) or to *Crafts Magazine* (with a focus on technique), and you would write it differently accordingly.

It is the same in sending out a proposal or requesting sponsorship. If someone is asking you to bid, find out as much as you can about them. If you are acting on your own initiative, a first step is to research companies (perhaps local) who might be responsive to suggestions. The box below has some suggested sources.

- Books and web sites (see also Part B, pages 119 and 133ff.).
- Local directories
- Donations and sponsorship yearbooks (Hollis Directories)
- *Who's Who* (A & C Black)
- Debrett's People of Today
- Key British Enterprises (Dun & Bradstreet)
- Marketing Manager's Yearbook (AP Information)
- KnowUK (Internet site available from major public libraries. See page 21).

These will have information on the marketing strategies of British businesses and may even tell you in what areas they are receptive to requests.

Then build a personal database on each organization that you plan to target. Look first for some points of reference or joint interest so that when you approach them with a request, you pitch it at the right level.

Have fields for specialisms, contact names, notes on meetings (as or if they occur) and any agreements reached.

Selling points

Are you asking for money or selling something that will be of
commercial benefit to the organization? You will be much
more successful with the second aim. Your sales technique
should stress the following points.

Publicity gains

Show how you intend to bring benefits to a wider audience
than those directly involved. This might be through media
attention, local business networks, Internet sites, open days,
speaking engagements, publication, or other activities. Spell
out how what you are doing applies to others, and indicate
how the funder's brand name will appear.

Value for money

Show that the funder is adding value, i.e. a really worthwhile
project would not go ahead at all, or would only go ahead more
slowly or on a lesser scale, without the funder's support. If they
feel it is worthwhile, and therefore makes them look good,
they may also think they are getting value for money.

Association with originality

Identify what is innovative or exciting about your project.
Maybe it's an original approach transferred to a different
forum; or that the way you are working with your partners is
something new. How might this bring about change? And how
might the funder benefit from that? A client likes to back
something unique. But you've got to show that what you offer
really *is* special, so check that it is and only use the word
'unique' if you mean 'one and no other'.

Remember
Failing to prepare is
preparing to fail.

Positivity

Say how your own enthusiasm and commitment will carry the
project through. Make the most of your own positive assets.

Verbal presentation

✖ *Don't!*

■ look greedy or
desperate.

■ try to be like
everyone else:
show that you
are different.

■ envy your
competitors'
strengths: try to
match them.

■ get angry in a
meeting.

■ forget to do your
homework.

Like the door-to-door salesman in chapter 1, your initial wish is to get your foot in the door and achieve a meeting. Whether this is possible or not often depends on the size of the project and whether you will be working together with other people. Make sure you know what dress is expected before the meeting. At the meeting, the client will probably expect a presentation—delivered by PowerPoint, storyboard, or flipchart.

PowerPoint

PowerPoint is the industry standard for computer presentations. It looks professional and you can show that you have done your homework without dwelling on every point. The disadvantage of PowerPoint is that people are often sitting in a darkened room staring straight ahead, so it tends to be better for a lecture-style presentation rather than an interactive one.

See also One Step
Ahead: Giving
Presentations by Jo
Billingham.

If you plan to use PowerPoint, or any other computer-based presentation software, do take a print-out with you as a back-up, just in case the technology does not work.

Storyboard

Advertising agencies often use the storyboard technique, using slogans and sketches on large boards so they can talk through the concept with the client. A storyboard—as the word implies—charts an idea in graphical form, showing a sequence of events. It allows you to interact directly with your audience as you unfold your idea and make it come alive before your group.

Flipchart

You can prepare a flipchart beforehand in the same way as you would create PowerPoint slides. Make sure you use thick, clearly visible pens and remember that your handwriting will

tell the client a great deal about you. Flipcharts are also useful
for brainstorming sessions—you can write down problems or
issues, and then jot down feedback on ideas and solutions as in
the diagram below. Using a flipchart interactively in front of an
audience you do not know requires a lot of self-confidence.

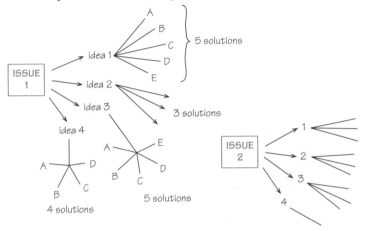

The presentation, like the proposal itself, needs to do these
things:

✔ Get attention.
Introduce yourself with an attention-grabbing opening.

✔ Say, 'This means you.'
Explain relevance to audience.

✔ Have a central message.
Give the general purpose of the project in as few words as
you can.

✔ Give examples.
Support your case with two or three examples, illustrations, or
personal stories.

✔ Close.
End on a striking sentence summarizing your presentation.

Finance

Pricing is the worst part—and varies from one type of bid to another. Do you ask for how much you need or how much it is worth to the client? And how do you quantify either of those?

Large funders
will not spend
time on
small fry.

As a first step, make sure that a selected client is in the right financial bracket for you—there is no point even applying to a funder who deals in multi-millions if you want the odd thousand. It is not administratively viable for large funders to spend time on small fry. They do not have petty purses to dispense small amounts, though you might think they could well afford it.

Then work out what you need as a minimum requirement to make the project viable. Work out how it might fund itself after that (if appropriate). You should also show what the financial risks of not doing the project might be.

The self-confident have no difficulty in putting forward realistically high bids; the modest will underestimate; the cautious will sensibly work out every detail and then stitch in some contingency (usually 10–20% of the whole).

Some tips

Asking for money is notoriously difficult in any circumstances. It will always depend a little on the people or organizations you are approaching. There aren't any 'correct' ways of doing it, but here are a few things to think about.

Tip
Ask for 90% of the funding before the event. And include the interest from that in your calculations.

Tip
Check and double-check that all your figures add up correctly.

- In your initial approach, you asked for financing within a 'from/to' range. Now it is time to ask for a specific sum of money. Be aware, though, that it is difficult to please all assessors. To some, round numbers look plucked out of the air; others look at a figure like £13,467.45 and think it looks too calculated. But if you ask for between £13,000 and £14,000, they will tend to offer you the lower figure. However, if the assessor feels the work entailed is worth a very great deal *more* than your quote, they could reject it on the grounds of being unrealistic.

■ If necessary, say that you are seeking a contribution of £X towards a total budget of £Y, and that you hope to raise the remainder from other sources, which you specify. Do not simply say that you are a very worthwhile organization and desperately need funds.

■ Don't forget about hidden costs like insurance, maintenance, and general overheads.

■ If you are sending a business plan as well, check that the figures are the same in all places.

See page 87.

■ In your breakdown of costs, identify these things, but do not put them in the initial quote—save them for the full application package (see chapter 4):

● travel expenses (mileage in the UK is usually between 25p and 40p a mile);

● maintenance costs whilst away (realistic, but modest);

● costs of administrative assistance (worked out on a daily or hourly rate);

● costs of consumable items (technical or other materials);

● hidden costs (insurance, heating);

● conference fees (or other attendances).

■ Your quotation should refer to the benefits and it is good to show you are open to negotiation with a phrase such as:

The opportunities in this proposal are neither comprehensive nor limiting, and we are happy to discuss alternatives and issue a further quotation to meet your requirements.

Costing your own time

It is difficult to cost your own time. The following formula to calculate the day rate of internal staff in a government office is a useful benchmark:

employee's annual salary + 50% divided by 210 (8 weeks holiday) = day rate

day rate ÷ 8 = hourly rate

This includes a contribution to cover routine overheads, e.g. computer costs, photocopying, telephone, and postage.

See also Part B, pages 116-7, for details on tax and invoicing.

If you use a formula like this, make sure your client realizes that routine overheads costs associated with the project are incorporated in the 50%.

For self-employed individuals, like craftsmen, performers, artists, conjurors, practitioners, and so on, the formula above does not work. The calculation runs like this:

A self-employed creative person working 40 hours a week estimates 75% of that time is productive. Allow 4 weeks for holiday and 2 weeks for sickness or down time.

40 hours x 75% = 30 hours

30 hours x 46 weeks = 1380 hours

Target income + yearly overheads ÷ 1380 = hourly rate

If it is a large project, and you will need outside help, it may be necessary to justify whom you intend to select for this. A rough rule of thumb (as used by government) suggests:

Value of work to be sub-contracted	Possible expectations of the client
up to £3,000	No need to justify choices
£3,000 to £20,000	Get at least three quotes from organizations
£20,000 and above	Initiate a full tendering exercise

Case study

As individuals, we can learn a lot from seeing how the giants operate. To put in context how the finances of large event sponsorship works, look at the way in which funding of the Football Association (FA) has expanded.

It first sold sponsorship rights to the England team in 1994. The initial sponsor was Green Flag, a vehicle breakdown company, which paid £4 million (Euro 2.6 million) over a four-season period ending with the World Cup in 1998. Nationwide then acquired the rights for the next four years for £15 million (Euro 22.8 million).

For the 2002–6 season, the FA expanded its number of funders to five, each contributing large amounts.

Carlsberg, Men's Sponsor
The deal worth £30 million (Euro 45.6 million) over four years provides Carlsberg with a shared association with the other partners for the national team and the FA Cup.

Nationwide Building Society, Women's Partner
The deal is also worth £30 million (Euro 45.6 million) over four years.

McDonald's, Community Sponsor
Also a deal of £30 million (Euro 45.6 million) for a four-year association.

Umbro, Elite Sponsor
They paid £140 million (Euro 217.5 million) for an eight-year partnership.

Pepsi UK, Youth Football
The four-year deal is worth £20 million (Euro 29.3 million).

To sum up . . .

Developing a campaign moves through these phases (not necessarily in this order):

1. Evidence that you understand the problem and agree priorities.
2. A realistic assessment of the timescale and what you can achieve within it.
3. Feasibility and details of the work plan.
4. Your ability to offer a range of possibilities.
5. Persuasive methodology and evaluation techniques.
6. Relevant experience from you and your colleagues.
7. Value for money.
8. Project costings with agreed milestones.
9. An effective dissemination strategy.
10. Commitment.

Tip
Winning proposals always demonstrate that the writer has *read the call for proposals thoroughly and carefully.*

4 The application package

Introduction

Your bid, proposal, or funding application will rarely be a single document; it will be a presentation package. All elements are worth considering, from the initial application form, or letter, to the reply card. Even the envelope.

This chapter will look at the elements below: it's best to read it in conjunction with the style details in chapter 5.

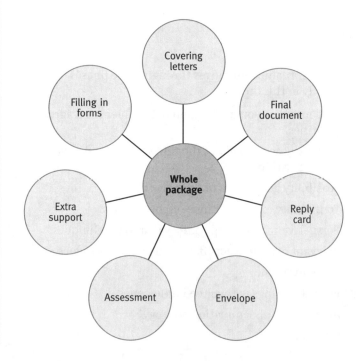

Application forms

Using forms

Some bids, proposals, or funding applications start with an application form. This is introductory information and need not include the complete package.

Look for guidelines that specify how to fill in the application forms. These should include:

- the eligibility criteria;

- the purpose of the bid, proposal, or funding application— who it will help and how, what is distinctive about it, what will be achieved;

- the financial procedures;

- the conditions for submitting an application;

- how much detail to give in each section.

If it asks you to describe an element of the proposal in no more than 100 words, make sure you really do stick to that. You should be able to convey the main flavour; if you've whetted their appetite, they will ask for more.

Sometimes an organization will positively encourage early preliminary submissions (which need not have all elements of the package at that stage) so that their trustees can give proper attention to the idea.

Submissions without forms

Not all submissions require an application form, but the funding organization may stipulate what information it requires. Treat their requirements in the same way as you would a form, by visualizing each requirement as a 'box' that you need to fill in. If there is none, then see if you can find advice from another similar organization and use that as your template.

Downloadable forms
Increasingly, grant-giving bodies are finding it economical to put application forms on a website. However, you may not be able to fill out the form online. This is because the form requires a signature or other supporting documentation. The form will be normally be downloadable from the site. Access to the Internet is a significant advantage.

The National Lottery has several dozen programmes and each has its own guidelines. Several of them run to 50 or 60 pages of advice and requests.

A sample requirement

The Carnegie UK Trust stipulates that all applications need the information listed below:

- Brief description of the organization—its history, work, budget, management, and staffing.

- Description of the project including its purpose; time scales incorporating any milestones during the programme; expected outcomes; number of people who will benefit; and how the project will be managed.

- Budget for the project, including details of funds already raised and other sources being approached.

- Amount requested from the Carnegie UK Trust.

- Plans for monitoring and evaluating the project. The Carnegie UK Trust attaches great importance to this.

- How the work will continue after the Carnegie UK Trust's grant has been completed.

- If appropriate, how it is proposed to share information about the project and what was learnt from it with others in the field.

See also the template and guidelines in Part B, pages 106–113.

- Last annual report, audited accounts, the main part of the signed constitution, charity registration number, and committee membership.

- Contact name, postal and email addresses, telephone and fax numbers. This should normally be the person directly responsible for the work, not a fundraiser. The application letter must be signed by the senior person responsible, such as the Chairman or the Director.

The presentation document

The length and components of a complete proposal document vary from project to project. The person reading it will scan it—as one does when reading a newspaper—looking for headlines, key issues, and summaries. So if you cut the document into sections with plenty of white space separating them and good clear headings, that helps the reader.

These are some possible sections.

See also the notes on structure on pages 38–9.

Part 1: Introductory

- Title page
- Contents list
- Project outline (also known as an Executive summary)

Part 2: Development

- Background
- Aims (or Rationale)
- Key concepts
- Development team
- Methodology
- Assumptions
- Activities
- Outcomes
- Rivals in the field (with comment)
- Timescale
- Resourcing implications (technical and personnel)
- Costings (with milestones)

See also 'Thinking through the objectives' on page 18.

Part 3: Conclusion

- Conclusion (or Recommendations)

Appendices

- Appendix 1: Curriculum Vitae of key team members
- Appendix 2: List of successful bids or similar projects
- Acknowledgements

Introductory

Title page

Even a four- or five-page proposal deserves a title page (or cover sheet), so your reader can see at a glance what it is. Spend some time in setting this out with attractive typography (incorporating your own logo if you have one). There may be a wizard in your word-processor to help you design this, though it looks fresher if you use it as the basis of your own template. The title page, and any section title pages, are the only parts of the document where the use of coloured paper looks good.

The title page generally includes:

- the name of the contact individual, together with telephone and fax numbers and email address;

- title of the proposal;

- details of any collaborating organisations;

- the current date—type this in yourself and do not let your word-processing package fill in an automatic date field because this will change each time the document is loaded.

For some projects it can also be useful to add a footer with:

- the total cost of the project;

- the timescale for completion;

- the bid number (where there is one).

See also the details in Part B, page 115.

Executive summary

Whether you label this as the Project outline, Abstract, Synopsis, or the Executive summary is up to you. The phrase has come into existence because busy company managers supposedly do not have time to read through an entire document and need the essence of it, at the top, in a single paragraph. This should distil the entire document: it is a précis of it. Write it last. This is the most important paragraph in the proposal document, and requires all your skills of brevity, clarity, and the ability to stress the salient points.

Development

We talked about the background thinking and planning in
chapters 1, 2, and 3. So you will already have notes and ideas to
arrange under the suggested headings on page 53. The order in
which you present them does not matter unduly. It is worth
making a few further remarks here, which have not been
covered earlier.

Financial statements

It depends on the level of detail you expect to go into at this
stage. If the project demands full financial figures, then it is a
great help to your reader if you give a commentary to the
costings. This could involve justification of the assumptions
behind the figures, a declaration that you are not looking for
any other funding, and other explanations.

See also page 46.

Conclusion

The conclusion (or list of recommendations) is the second place
your reader will turn to after having read the executive
summary. They may not read anything else, so do be aware that
these two sections have to contain everything you want the
reader to know. You will probably give a two-line version of the
conclusion in the covering letter as well. Here is where you can
expand on it and impress the reader with the full weight of
your argument and ideas.

Appendices

The information in the appendices is 'extra' and serves to
establish your credentials and impress the client. If you are at
the beginning of your career, think about other ways of doing
the same thing. A CV full of school achievements and work
experience may not serve you well and is best not offered
unless requested. Inexperience need not count against you; try
to discover (and offer) your positive assets.

Covering letter

The covering letter is critical. It is what people will read first. And it is here that an individual voice can come through.

Tip
The Debrett site <http://www.debretts.co.uk/> tells you the correct form of address for people with titles. The correct mode of address to MPs is at <http://www.parliament.uk/>.

Make it long enough to say what you want, but short enough to be easy to take in at a skim reading. This can be a tall order. Market research has shown that a request can fail if is too long and the recipient can't be bothered to wade through it, and it can fail because the writer didn't convey enough for the recipient to feel like acting.

There is a cultural divide here. In the UK, standard advice is to keep to a single page for your main letter. In the US, a four-page letter is quite normal. My own preference is for a short, friendly letter introducing yourself and your request with additional matter as enclosures (listed at the end of the letter). This can be anything from a leaflet to a full-blown proposal document in a presentation folder.

Do not send more than you need at any one stage. For example, if you want to find a publisher for a book, you would send the contents page, a brief synopsis, and possibly a chapter of the text itself. You would not send the whole book until the editor requested it.

The same applies to fund-raising letters, bids, and proposals of all hues. Give the client what they have asked for—if they have asked for anything at all. Give no more and no less.

The opener

See page 73 for some useful phrases to use in your covering letter.

The reader must know what you want within the first two sentences. Opposite are some examples of 'proposals' I have received in one week. They all come from organizations who probably have professional fund raisers working for them, so you and I should be able to learn something from them. After all, they have teams of market researchers telling them how direct marketing works. Direct marketing is a useful parallel for your own sponsorship and fund-raising letters for an activity, event, or study time.

Let's look at the opening 'gambit'—the move by which they hope to hook a prospective client. I'll add how I reacted to each one. See if you agree.

Visit Scotland

Before you do anything else, make a note of this telephone number [*given*] because you're going to want to dial it. When you call, we'll simply take your details and send you out a copy of VisitScotland's Autumn Gold brochure. And once it arrives, you won't be disappointed. It's simply bursting with goodness—the rich harvest of offers to tempt you—and it's the starting point for an unforgettable short break in one of the finest destinations in the world: Scotland.

Unnecessary as there is a form enclosed as well.

A mistake to suggest negativity.

Rich harvest sounds nice.

Here's the pitch: they want me to visit Scotland. Why don't they start with that?

Dear Theatregoer,

I hope that you enjoyed your recent visit to Shakespeare's Globe Theatre. We have been thrilled to be welcoming capacity audiences to each performance.

You may already be aware that the Shakespeare's Globe is more than a theatre, and this is my purpose in writing to you today—to tell you more about our many other areas of activity and, I hope, to secure your support for the exciting opportunities that are ahead of us.

They are colluding with me and forming a partnership.

Have you? So what?

Now I know we are getting to the point.

My curiosity is aroused and I know they are now going to tell me what these are. I am having to wait a long time to find out how much it will cost me.

Trying to draw me in.

This is a good beginning — they have come straight out with what they want.

The rationale.

The pitch.

Dear Friend,

Can you help PDSA?

PDSA treats over 4,500 sick and injured pets every day for owners who cannot afford vet's fees and qualify for help. That costs over £27 million (Euro 42.8 million) a year and we received no grants from the National Lottery or support from the government for our veterinary services. In fact we rely on support from the public.

That is why we are asking you to sell or buy as many of the Grand Draw tickets as you can. Each book of tickets raises £5. As little as £10 could save the life of a much-loved pet.

The middle

The body (and bulk) of the letter should flesh out your opener and add extra detail. The PDSA letter, quoted above, goes on like this:

Doing so much good could bring you a reward.

There are 17 prizes to win in the October Draw including a £7,000 first prize. The knowledge that you have helped sick animals is rewarding in itself—when you could win a superb prize too, simply by caring, how can you lose?

See also
'Transitional phrases'
and 'Sign-offs' on
pages 73 and 78.

In a letter accompanying a full-blown proposal, you could explain what is in the rest of the package and why each item is enclosed. The reader can see the rationale at a glance and decide what to look at next.

Reading through the letter

Read it as if you were the person it is pitched at, and ask yourself these questions:

■ Was the purpose of the letter clear?

■ Did it persuade or inform you?

- Did it make any assumptions about you as a reader?

- How many ideas are being communicated?

- Could it be shorter?

- Did it seem authoritative?

- Was there anything ambiguous, or phrased in such a way that someone might misunderstand?

- Can you tell whether any parts of this letter were cut and pasted from somewhere different?

- Is the spelling and grammar impeccable?

There are several books in the One Step Ahead series to help you with spelling and grammar if neither is a strong point. At the very least, use your word-processor's inbuilt checker for any inadvertent errors, and do this right at the end when you have finished the documentation. Silly errors creep in so easily. There is a mind-set that responds to errors with the thought, 'If they can't get that right, can they do the project?' It need not be true, but isn't worth the risk.

> **Did you know?**
> Spelling errors are known as 'spoilers'.

Referee's letter

By a referee, I mean someone who will give you a good testimonial to give a boost to your application. For example, if you are looking for support for community funding (a sports event, an arts venue, a social outing, or whatever it is) then would it enhance your application package if it contained a short letter from a prominent local citizen? Success breeds success, so if you can demonstrate that one key person is willing to give support, others are more likely to follow.

On the other hand, if this is an application for private advancement of some kind, then don't include full references unless you have been specifically asked to give them. The aim is to keep your application package lean and mean, and interesting enough so they request further details from you.

> **Usage**
> **Re**
> Strictly speaking **re** should be used in headings and references, as in *Re Ainsworth versus Chambers*, but not as a normal word meaning 'regarding', as in *thanks for your letter re TSB*. However the evidence suggests that **re** is now widely used in the second context, and is now generally accepted.
>
> *New Oxford Dictionary of English*

Reply card

Always include a stamped addressed envelope as it will increase the probability of a response. Or would your application or project benefit from a reply card? One of your aims, remember, is to make life easy for your opposite number. It may make all the difference between a response and your application languishing at the bottom of someone's in-tray. Here are some examples of circumstances in which a reply card may be useful.

Application for a grant

> Dear Jane,
>
> Thank you for your application materials for XYZ.
>
> Tick as appropriate:
>
> ☐ We are pleased to tell you that you have been successful and we will contact you further in due course.
>
> ☐ Unfortunately, you have not been successful in your proposal for XYZ and the reason was that
>
> ....
> ....
>
> Yours sincerely,

Keep this vague so the recipient has to think of something to say. You do not want to put negative ideas in their heads; on the other hand, you learn from feedback.

Incentive offer

Offering an incentive can work in limited circumstances. People like the idea of getting something for nothing. You must remember that there are laws governing how these operate. For example, if you want to sell raffle tickets by post you must register with the local authority. Ring up your local Council and ask for the Licensing department. They will send you a form and guidance notes. Each ticket must cost no more than

£1, have the name and address of the promoter on it, the price, the date of the draw, the fact that you are registered with the local authority, and registered under the Lottery and Amusement Act 1976, and a registration number.

Date as postmark

☐ Yes, I would like to enter the XYZ Prize Draw for

[*Attractive and appropriate incentive*]

in support of the [*Your cause in a nutshell*]

☐ I enclose the ticket book with names filled in and the collected sum of £___

Raffle tickets help to generate funding as the recipient feels they might get some return. This approach is no good for a business or foundation. Think what other incentives you can offer.

Response to a fund-raising letter

Date as postmark

✓ Yes, I'd like to support the XYZ project. Please enrol me as a:

Tick as appropriate

☐ Gold member at £XXX

☐ Silver member at £YYY

☐ Bronze member at £ZZZ

☐ I don't want to become a member, but I will give you £___

☐ I enclose a cheque for my tax-deductible contribution made payable to XYZ Events

☐ Please debit my tax-deductible contribution from:

Card type: Visa / Switch / Mastercard

Credit card number:

Expiry date: Start date:

Signature:

Try and be inventive with 'types' of membership. Make them appropriate to your project. Try to make each level equally attractive. Spell out again what they would get at each level.

Credit card payments are easiest for users, but are not appropriate for small groups or individuals.

Envelope

Multiple mailing

I throw a lot of direct mail letters unopened in the bin because of the envelope. You can see instantly that it is an appeal. You can often see who from. I particularly dislike the ones that send a coin or a Biro in the expectation that I will open the envelope and read on.

Some envelopes are emblazoned with teasers—half sentences that are cute, provocative, or make promises, e.g.:

You'll be glad you opened this

Your membership enclosed

Free gift inside

Sensational Savings

Stop! Don't throw this in the bin

Open carefully . . . a free spirit is inside

THIS IS NOT A CIRCULAR

This is the story—the long and true story—of one ocean, two ships, and 150 men.

It is quite easy, with modern printers, to print individual messages or even small pictures, on the envelope, but do you want to expend that extra effort? Everyone's psychology is different, but for me free gifts and envelope teasers are a turn-off. I feel guilty and guilt is not a good way of initiating a relationship. Giving money—to charity or for any other reason—should be a relationship where both parties feel good.

For individuals seeking sponsorship, it is easier—and I think better—to stick to a plain envelope with the individual's name on it (and make sure it is spelled correctly) with a second-class stamp. Everyone knows (even if you personalize) that sponsorship letters are sent in the dozens or the hundreds.

First class could raise doubts. Are you profligate (if you aren't economical; will you spend their money wisely) or inefficient (if you're in a hurry, is it because you haven't planned in advance properly)?

If you have a good hand, handwritten envelopes are better than printer labels especially where you have taken the trouble to make an individualized approach. A nicely-written envelope also conveys something of your character and people like that. Labels instantly say it's a mass mailing. So do window envelopes.

Some applicants try to seize attention with bright red or green envelopes. Coloured envelopes shout too loudly and can be counter-productive as you look over-eager, if not a little desperate. There's nothing wrong with the subtle elegance of white.

Single mailing

If you are responding to a bid or call for proposals, you will not be mass mailing and how you send it is not an issue. Hand delivery can be effective and gives peace of mind. Otherwise, make sure any large envelope containing a complete folder protects the package. You may be asked to put a reference code on the envelope. Check if this is necessary.

If, for any reason, your proposal is sensitive to copyright (you fear your words, scenarios, or story-boarding might be used without acknowledgment to you), send it by registered mail and send a copy of the complete package to yourself by registered mail and do not open it. It's an extreme measure, but should there be cause for dispute, you will have date-stamped proof of your work having been sent to a client before they 'borrowed' your work. This does, unfortunately, happen. Sometimes a client may like the ideas in your proposal, but wants to work with another supplier. An ethical client will negotiate a fee with you for that. For the sake of future working relationships, it can be sensible to agree to this, especially as there is no copyright in ideas—only in the expression of them, i.e. the way you write them down. A treatment, or scenario, or proposal can come perilously close to an 'expression' of ideas.

Did you know?
Stephen Joyce, who manages the James Joyce estate, will only read hand-written applications and will only respond if he likes your handwriting.

Tip
Establish copyright through registered post.

Packaging

Take some care over the binder in which you send the package. Make sure the pages turn easily, and that they don't fall out. Consider whether to have a transparent acetate cover so that the details on the title page are instantly obvious, or whether to repeat some of them.

If you have a company (or personal) folder, it is a good idea to use it for image branding, or to convey extra subliminal information. For example, your folder might have a list of previous sponsors with their logos, which conveys to the client that you are responsible about acknowledging sources without drawing attention to this yourself. Or it may convey in graphic or pictorial form more about the organization for whom you are making the bid.

We asked Monsoon why they chose us and they said it was because we put a flower on the cover of the proposal.

Motivation workshop leader

After all, everyone will come to a pitch with a set of headings very like the ones on page 53. How do you differentiate yourself so you stand out from the rest as someone special? The quality of your ideas, naturally, counts for a great deal. No amount of packaging will disguise woolly thinking. But feel-good factor is certainly influential. It also shows you care about detail and that makes the client think you will care about the intricacies of what they need.

Emailing

Don't send in a complete proposal by email unless you know the people very well and are 100% certain that they are happy to handle it that way. For one thing, you cannot be certain that a document you send as an attachment will print out the way you want it to. Even if the recipient has the same version of the same word-processor as you have, it will recompose itself slightly for different printers.

Assessing the package

Think of the complete package as a decathlon in which you are competing. You have to be strong in all areas, not just one.

Remember, if you are one of many applicants, the recipient will welcome almost anything that makes it easier to reject one that doesn't match up to expectations. Conditions under which bids, proposals, or funding applications may be rejected include:

- not submitted on the correct forms;

- price unreasonable (low or high);

- signature missing;

- failure to meet requirements;

- not received in time;

- sent by fax or email;

- conflict of interest.

Don't let something trivial spoil the rest.

When you have assembled all the parts of the package that are relevant to your particular bid, proposal, or funding application, look through it and see how you rate it against the criteria on the following page. If possible, ask someone else to do this as well. A second and third opinion is always valuable.

Before you send it

Go through your documents and put a tick in the margin by every up-beat or positive statement and a cross beside anything that could be read negatively or with the voice of caution. Count the ticks and crosses at the end. If there are more minuses than you'd imagined, it could detract from the overall enthusiasm. See if you can convert any crosses to ticks.

 Turn-offs

- multiple applications from the same person addressed to different people in a company
- inability to spell
- people who don't read the guidelines
- people who are not sure what they want to do
- pretentious, overblown statements.

 Turn-ons

- professional presentations
- enthusiasm about the project
- practical costings
- realistic timeframes.

Circle your own assessment rating of the complete package on a scale of 5 = best, 0 = worst.

Criterion	Rating	Weight	Total
Emphasizes benefits to the recipient, not your needs.	0 1 2 3 4 5	× 4 =	
Asks for a specific sum of money (or range) or required action at the beginning; costs represent value for money.	0 1 2 3 4 5	× 3 =	
Repeats this request (differently worded) at the end.	0 1 2 3 4 5	× 2 =	
Speaks directly to the reader; uses 'I' and 'You', and addresses a named individual.	0 1 2 3 4 5	× 2 =	
Is easy to read; uses simple language, short paragraphs, no jargon; uses active tense.	0 1 2 3 4 5	× 3 =	
Looks attractive: nicely spaced; printed with clear title page carrying your name; contents list; presentation folder or binding if appropriate.	0 1 2 3 4 5	× 2 =	
All pages have a header or footer with page numbers and the individual or organization's name.	0 1 2 3 4 5	× 1 =	
Fulfils all requirements in the guidelines (or as on pages 104–111 if none given).	0 1 2 3 4 5	× 4 =	
Contains all necessary supporting documentation including a short, friendly covering letter.	0 1 2 3 4 5	× 1 =	
Is within a given deadline, or allows plenty of leeway for time-related occurrences.	0 1 2 3 4 5	× 2 =	
Has realistic objectives and financial calculations.	0 1 2 3 4 5	× 5 =	
Makes it easy for the recipient to respond (e.g. reply card, SAE, email address).	0 1 2 3 4 5	× 1 =	
Your score Total the 12 ratings remembering to multiply by the weighting. The maximum score is 150 points. To see how you did, see the evaluation in the margin.			

Score Results:
140–150 Excellent
120–139 Extremely good
110–129 Very good
90–109 Good
55–89 Room for improvement
30–54 Needs quite a lot more work
0–29 Perhaps you'd better start again

Follow-up enquiry

A follow-up letter continues a dialogue. But you don't want to nag or come across as too anxious. So how long to leave it before you write in and enquire about an application from which you have heard nothing?

That's a 'how long is a piece of string?' question as some things are time-sensitive and some are not. If you know you are one of many pitching for the same thing, and that there is a set deadline, then consider enclosing a stamped addressed envelope in your application, or a reply card like the one on page 60.

As a guide...
A government department requesting bids in September is unlikely to reply before the following January.

A reply card makes it easy for the client to respond. Failing that, try an email enquiry the day after you know they have made up their minds. That is very easy for the responder too. Wait a bit, though, as the chances are that they will contact you immediately if you have won the bid. It depends how big a bid it is, and how much is at stake.

Give an email message an obvious subject line, so it doesn't get instantly deleted, e.g.:

Subject: Jane Dorner's Application for XYZ

You could begin by asking whether they have reached a decision as expected. They may have told you to expect a decision on the 1st of the following month, but may have all sorts of reasons for being unable to meet that date.

If the project has no particular 'sell-by date' then wait as long as you feel is reasonable. If you have put forward a proposal to a publisher for a book, for example, three months of silence would not be beyond their pale. You fear that prodding them at all will lead to instant rejection as it is the quickest way of dealing with the matter. Try to think of a gentle reminder that will not make the person at the other end feel guilty that they have not got back to you.

Additional documents

The client or funder may come back to you for more
documents. Don't assume you get black marks because you
didn't supply them first time round. It is a good sign and means
you are past a first hurdle. The things they might ask for
(especially for larger applications) include:

- a business plan;

- more detailed costings;

- a more detailed timetable for the work;

- job descriptions, work plans, software specifications;

- your Constitution (or Memorandum & Articles of
  Association, etc.);

- your equal opportunities policy;

- letters of support from other organizations.

It isn't a bad idea if you enclose a list of other documents that
you could offer if you write a follow-up letter. At least it will
show them that you do have a business plan, or policies on
such things as equal opportunities (or privacy or health and
safety). Such things count for a lot for some funders. Of course,
this does not apply to individuals, but small businesses should
have these things. If yours is a start-up company, and you are
looking for seed-corn funding, then it might be an idea to make
a start on creating the above documentation before a possible
funder puts you on the spot by asking for it.

Thank you letter

Don't forget the thank you letter. It is never a mistake to thank
people for their support, their patronage, for what the
partnership with them is going to achieve, or just to say you
look forward to working together.

It is the small contributions that people often forget to
acknowledge—the £25 towards a local concert; the £50 for a
sports venture; or £5 towards a commemorative park seat. No
offering is too small for a letter of thanks. They won't give

again if they don't get an adequate 'pat on the back'. Your letter should make them feel they count as much as anyone else. One person's £5 is another person's £5,000.

If your bid is unsuccessful, it is still useful to write a thank you letter appreciating the time spent considering your application. Ask if you can apply again some other time, and whether you might phone to talk about ways you could improve your proposal when approaching other potential partners. In that conversation, you could also see if they will recommend another possible partner.

To sum up . . .

Consider every element of the application package with the same enthusiasm and attention to detail:

1. Is there an application form and have you filled in all details requested?

2. What section and paragraph divisions will you have in your presentation document? Do the headings convey exactly what will follow?

3. Is there an executive summary?

4. Do you repeat the main request in the conclusion?

5. Have you spent enough time on the covering letter? It is the most important item in the whole package.

6. Is it appropriate to include a reply card?

7. Have you given thought to the appearance of the whole package and the envelope it is in?

8. What additional documents should you include at first proposal stage and are there others that you can offer to send later?

9. Have you remembered to:

   ■ review Terms and Conditions (if given);

   ■ sign the bid or letter in ink;

   ■ complete the delivery information;

   ■ review and complete all requirements listed to ensure bid compliance?

Divide information into:
- must know
- should know
- nice to know.

5 | Style detail

That is why in my party conference speech I said that my three priorities for government would be education, education, and education.

Tony Blair (December 1996)

Cultivating brevity

When you are describing your aims, objectives, and public image, it is vital to be brief and precise. Every book in the One Step Ahead series emphasizes the need for this in functional writing, and you will find much about style in each book. Here are some common tips:

- Say less—read through for redundancy (see below).

- Use lists—vertical lists break up sequences into manageable chunks (as illustrated throughout this book).

- Keep the flow—connect sentences with link words or phrases (as on page 74).

- Be positive—there's no need to qualify every statement to take account of every possible circumstance. It's not a legal document and readers can adapt. See page 75.

- Avoid jargon, newspeak, and cliché—see page 76.

- Don't be wordy—omit complicated sentences with too many words; use one word instead of two or three. See page 77.

- Split sentences—break long sentences into shorter ones for easy readability.

- Eliminate ambiguity—read carefully and if someone could misunderstand, rewrite the sentence.

Repetition

Remember to distinguish between useful repetition and useless redundancy. To get a point across, you may have to say it several times in different ways throughout a long document. Repetition is a rhetorical ploy often used by public speakers. Just make sure you aren't saying the same thing twice on the same page.

Ensuring readability

The eyes don't read; they move across a line of print in a series of jerks and pauses. During the pauses the eyes take a 'photograph'. When the eyes come to a full stop, the brain organizes the photographs so that the message makes sense. If the brain comes across something it doesn't understand, it will instruct the eyes to 're-photograph'. If this happens a lot, the reader will give up and move on to something else.

As someone with a mission to sell, you want to keep their eyes on your page. How? There are many ways, of course, but it helps to bear these tips in mind:

- Put yourself in the reader's shoes.
- Plan a beginning, middle, and end.
- Use the first person and address your reader as 'you'.
- Write as you speak.
- Write about people, things, and facts.
- Be brief, but not so brief that it lacks colour.
- Use the active voice. 'I did this,' not 'This was done to me.'
- Be specific. Use illustrations, case studies, and examples.
- Start a new sentence for each new idea.
- Keep sentences and paragraphs short, and signpost each chunk with clear, descriptive headings rather than quirky or clever ones.
- Use direct questions. Then answer them.
- Avoid spoilers (such as poor grammar) which undermine credibility.
- Avoid ambiguity, jargon, and heavy-handed attempts at humour.
- Arrange the writing interestingly on the page.

Writing is the hardest way of earning a living, with the possible exception of wrestling with alligators.

Olin Miller

Selling benefits

This book has indicated several times the importance of spelling out the benefits. That means being very specific about the way you phrase what those gains are. Talk about measurable benefits, not about features. For example:

A **feature** (e.g. flat screen).

A **benefit** (e.g. means you use less space and power).

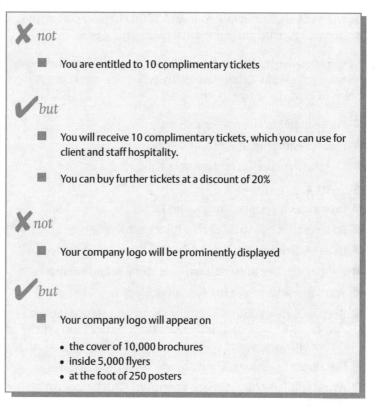

✗ *not*

■ You are entitled to 10 complimentary tickets

✔ *but*

■ You will receive 10 complimentary tickets, which you can use for client and staff hospitality.

■ You can buy further tickets at a discount of 20%

✗ *not*

■ Your company logo will be prominently displayed

✔ *but*

■ Your company logo will appear on

- the cover of 10,000 brochures
- inside 5,000 flyers
- at the foot of 250 posters

Starter phrases

In the section on the covering letter (page 56) I emphasized the importance of first impressions. Don't struggle with your opening sentence as you can always change it later. Remember ingenuity doesn't raise money, but directness does. It is usually wiser and more productive than subtlety. If you don't know how to begin your letter, try one of these stock phrases:

- I am writing to you today because . . .

- You may be surprised to learn . . .

- Did you know that . . .

- Do you wish . . .

- I want to tell you a story about . . .

- I am writing to invite you . . .

- If you've always wanted to . . .

- It's hard to believe, but . . .

- I think you'll be interested in this unusual . . .

- I know you support XYZ, so . . .

- As you have been so generous in the past . . .

Transitional phrases

A transition is a word or phrase that links two sentences. It keeps the reader's attention on track. Like a Highway Code marking; it signposts small twists and turns in the road in advance so the reader can prepare to change gear or direction. On the next page are some useful phrases and the types of guidance they give the reader.

The secret of a well-written bid, proposal, or funding application (any piece of writing in fact) is 'flow'. If each sentence flows seamlessly to the other and each paragraph leads on logically from the one before, the reader will follow the argument. The structure must be right for that to occur. Even so, link phrases (like the one that begins this sentence) help to join one line of thought to another in a smooth flow.

I used to know someone who held that if you had to start a sentence with the word, 'Moreover', then it was a weak sentence and needed rewriting. I agree up to a point. I have nothing against transitional link phrases, but if you can take them out again as you edit without losing any of the flow or meaning, then you will probably strengthen the writing. Overuse of link words diminishes their impact.

Usage
And . . . or . . .
Where a verb follows a list separated by 'or', the traditional rule is that the verb should be singular, as in: *a sandwich* **or** *other snack is included in the price.* The argument is that each of the elements agrees separately with the verb. The opposite rule applies when the elements are joined by **and**: here, the verb should be plural: *a sandwich* **and** *a cup of coffee are included in the price.*

New Oxford Dictionary of English

73

Addition

And
Also
As well as
Besides
Furthermore
Including
In addition
Moreover
Too

Cause and effect

As
As a result
Because
Consequently
Even if
For
Given that
If
On account of
On the assumption
Since
Therefore
Thus
With this in mind

Contrast

All the same
But
Even so
However
In spite of
Nevertheless
That said
To some extent
Yet

Comparison

Although
Similarly
Likewise
In the same way
Just as . . . so . . .

Illustration

For example
For instance

In other words
Specifically
That is
To clarify

Involving the reader

Ask yourself
As I'm sure you'll
    understand
Before I tell you
It's people like you who
Let me explain
Supposing
Think of it:

Place

Alongside
At this point
Below
Here
Next to
On the next page
Opposite
There

Sequence

First
Next
After
Before
Ultimately
Finally
So far

Time

But now, for the first
    time
Currently
Earlier
Later
Meanwhile
Now
Now is the time to
Then
To date
Today, more than ever,
Until
Up to now
Why wait

Being positive

Choose your words to give positive signals. Compare the words in the table. If you were a business, which column would you be keen to associate yourself with? Think about the words that apply to your specific project and see if you can 'up-sell' any that make you look like a risky proposition.

✗ Negative	✓ Positive
small	focused
controversial	imaginative
minority	exclusive
experimental	original
precarious	exciting
hazard	opportunity

Other positive signals:

- Always use the word 'will' rather than 'would' because that makes the project seem real, rather than something that you are thinking about doing.

- Refer to the project by its full name when writing the proposal—you might have used an abbreviation that you understand, but that your reader might not.

- Spell out acronyms. If the reader is likely to know them, spell them out on first use and put the shortened form in brackets afterwards. Then use the acronym only after that. If there are lots of them, provide a list in the appendices.

- Spell out your company name each time it is mentioned (instead of using a shortened form) to show you are proud of it, and to fix it in the reader's mind.

- Ask a colleague to read your application to check that the proposal makes sense, that you have not made assumptions that the bid-evaluator will not understand, and that you have developed the bid logically.

Vague language

A mass of Latin
words falls
upon the facts
like soft snow,
blurring the
outline and
covering up all
the details. The
great enemy of
clear language
is insincerity.
When there is
a gap between
one's real and
one's declared
aims, one turns
as it were
instinctively to
long words and
exhausted
idioms, like a
cuttlefish
spurting out
ink.

George Orwell

Jargon

Bids and proposals, like other forms of business writing, suffer from the use of ready-made phrases, over-used idioms, mixed metaphors, stale clichés, and wordy imprecision. Writers grasp at fashionable phrases without always thinking about them, or visualizing the word pictures they make.

It may be because, in writing a bid, the task is to convert abstract ideas into words. This is not easy—people who have entrepreneurial ideas often have difficulty putting them into words. It helps to know that you are not alone, and that even established writers struggle with words and phrases. One needs to be constantly vigilant, reading through and asking, 'Is this what I really mean?' and 'Could someone else misunderstand what I am saying?'

You can help your reader (who will then be better disposed towards your proposal) by cutting out short-hand phrases associated with your own work. Some specialist language comes across as jargon to those who do not work in the same field. Sometimes it really *is* jargon. Consider the phrases in the top box opposite.

Wordy phrases

Similarly, it is a common fault to think that long sentences dressed up with pretentious wording sound impressive. They don't. They hide real meaning under a blanket of verbiage.

If you look at the bottom box opposite, you will notice that we often use four or five words where one will do. The words in the right-hand column are almost always better. But you cannot be rigid about it. Sometimes a sentence sounds better with a longer phrase. So trust your judgement, but try to avoid stock phrases simply because you haven't noticed how wordy they are.

Fashionable phrases	Plain meaning
24/7	all the time
bleeding, leading, or cutting edge	up-to-date
bottom out	get as low as it can get
execute on	do
finalize	complete
flavour of the month	popular
funds	money
input	ideas, contribution
in receipt of	have received
interface	meet, talk to
make a judgement call	decide
measurable outcomes	specific aims
parameters	limits
prior to	before
purchase	buy
pushing out the envelope	challenging constraints
singing from the same hymn sheet	working together
streamline	reduce
think outside the box	be imaginative
utilize	use
viral marketing	word-of-mouth
window	space in the diary

Wordy	Simple
a wide range of	many
along the lines of	like
at an early date in the future	soon
at this moment in time	now
due to the fact that	because
few and far between	few
I am not in a position to	I cannot
in the event that	if
in view of the fact that	since
is in our possession	we have
it came to light	we found
it is our understanding that	we understand that
this affords us the opportunity	this allows us
we are of the opinion that	we believe
with regard to	about
with the result that	so that

The sign-off

End by rephrasing your request in as few words as you possibly can. When you have done that, cut it shorter again. The ending is as important as the opening, and will vary according to the type of project.

For proposals

Ending by saying, 'I look forward to hearing from you,' is a little lame. It puts the onus on the other person to do something, and they won't like that. It is better to keep the initiative and end by saying:

> I will contact your office in a few days'/weeks' time to ask what you thought of this proposal, and I hope we will be able to meet soon after that.

If there is a deadline date in the call, then you could indicate that you have noted and understood that, e.g.:

> Thank you for reading this proposal and I hope to have good news from you on, or soon after, [date/month].

For funding or charity requests

If you respond within X days, you'll receive . . .

Your gift of $X makes it possible for us to . . .

And remember, your gift is tax deductible . . .

All it takes to . . . is for you to send . . .

$X is just . . . per day . . .

Don't miss this chance to . . .

What seems like a small gift to you can seem . . .

For less than a cup of coffee a day, you can . . .

Thousands of people will suffer unless you . . .

American studies suggest that people read the P.S. in a direct mail letter first. Whether they do or not, it is hard to say, but it stands out from the rest and it can be useful for your repeat pitch to go there. Americans call this 'the ask'. In the margin are some examples (from US sources).

You'll notice that these all use a measure of emotional blackmail (especially the last). This may be appropriate, but think about the tone of each one. It's best not to be too desperate. Try to end on a positive note. Maybe even with a simple, 'Thank you'.

Don't forget, as signee, to sign. Failure to do so is another give-away of sloppiness or inattention (and frequently occurs in mass-mailing). Print your name as well, and, if appropriate, give a title so that it is clear what your role in the organization is.

Combining charts and graphics with text

When you turn the pages of this book, do you concentrate on the words alone, or do the pictures influence you? Do they amuse you? distract you? puzzle you? add to your understanding?

Illustrations, in their original sense, were pictures that illustrated the text, as in 'showing something in the text again'. Today, we live in a more image-led society and the image frequently replaces the text.

The One Step Ahead series has a policy on how it uses illustrations and how they enhance the message. To some extent this is an individual affair; people respond to pictures in their own way. For some, a flow chart really pin-points whole paragraphs; others find them confusing. Pictures are read in a different way to text because their logic depends on space and on elements in relationships with each other. The eye takes in an image more quickly, but it may interpret it individually, so if you decide to use graphic elements, do so sparingly.

Choose between:
- photograph
- cartoon
- line diagram
- bar chart
- pie chart
- table
- Gantt chart
- flow chart.

If your answer to the questions below is 'yes', then an image will probably serve you well:

▪ Is there a photo of a physical object that I can show instead of describing it?

▪ Will a cartoon lighten the message?

▪ Am I comparing one total with other totals?

▪ Am I showing change over a period of time?

▪ Do I want to show a figure as a proportion of the whole?

Let's look at each of these and see how graphics help to show what may otherwise be buried in a mass of wordiness.

Photographs and diagrams

Remember the adage, 'Show don't tell'? If you are fund-raising for third world poverty, a picture will have more impact than any words. Similarly, certain types of proposal may depend on the reader being able to visualize what you are talking about. Use pictures in such cases; otherwise do not.

Cartoon

The cartoons in this book are (I think) delightful and wittily amplify the points they lampoon. Bids and proposals are not, however, publication documents, and there is no need to go to the expense of commissioning drawings. On a charity mail-shot, however, you might use one or two—but make sure the style is finely tuned to your audience. Taste in cartoon characters is highly individual.

Line diagram

Helps readers to visualize quantities, plotted over a period of time by using a rising or falling line. Usually there is an x-axis (vertical scale) representing quantity and a y-axis (horizontal scale) representing time. A line joins together points plotted on a grid (often a curve). Line diagrams are useful for showing financial statements or any set of figures with a flow that needs to be shown over a period of time. You can show one, two, or three lines, but more is just confusing.

See also One Step Ahead: Presenting Numbers, Tables, and Charts by Sally Bigwood and Melissa Spore.

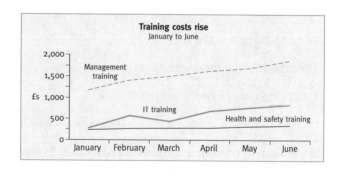

Bar chart

Useful for visualization of quantities, each one represented by individual bars or columns showing the amount counted. This is useful for giving prominence to individual figures rather than to the overall picture or to a comparison of different elements. You can arrange items on bar charts horizontally or vertically (and because readers read from left to right, the horizontal arrangement often works best).

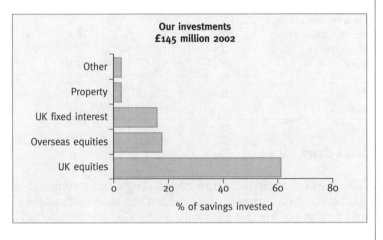

Pie chart

The division of a whole into its components, usually at percentages of a circle. This is useful to show up to 8 component parts of the whole, and is often used for showing budget comparisons, market figures, and analysis of income or of spending. The eye automatically reads a pie chart clockwise, starting at twelve o'clock position. So if you want to emphasize one particular cake slice, start with this segment at the top and continue round. Show the most important slice in the darkest shade.

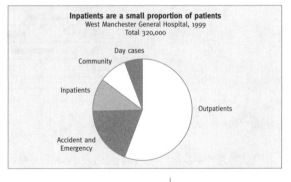

Table

Displays numbers or words arranged in columns and is useful for timetables, calendars, distance, and budget figures.

Agents lead our sales
Value of sales orders by region and source, 2002 (£ thousands)

	Agents	Franchises	Website	Travel shops	Average
London and south	35	60	11	8.2	28
Scotland and NI	33	41	11	9.8	24
Midlands and Wales	49	18	19	7.7	23
North	39	22	11	7.5	20
Outside Europe	35	6.7	10	5.5	14
Europe	26	11	7.1	4.5	12
Average	36	26	11	7.2	

Gantt chart

This type of chart shows a timeline and is useful for time management on a project so your client can see clearly where your milestones are and how you are blocking out the allotted time.

Flow chart

Gives a staged overview of the steps in a process or project and can either be read logically from left to right, or with arrows leading the eye around the page. It is best if you avoid putting too much information in a flow chart. Thought processes that are very clear to you may confuse your reader at first sight. The golden rule is: the less information you include on any chart, the easier it is to follow.

Some of these are easy to produce in Microsoft Office packages, and there are a number of different effects that you can achieve. There is also free software on the Internet to help you create charts of all kinds.

Tip
Try free trials or shareware at:
www.smartdraw.com
or
www.tucows.com.

To sum up . . .

Are there any rules?

This is a chapter on style and the final word must be that rules are made to be broken.

As a general rule, run your pen through every other word you have written; you have no idea what vigour it will give your style.

Sydney Smith

A good writer will always trust natural instinct rather than relying on rules of grammar. George Orwell says in his essay *Politics and the English Language* (1946):

A scrupulous writer, in every sentence that he writes, will ask himself at least four questions, thus:

1. What am I trying to say?
2. What words will express it?
3. What image or idiom will make it clearer?
4. Is this image fresh enough to have an effect?

And he will probably ask himself two more:

1. Could I put it more shortly?
2. Have I said anything that is avoidably ugly?

Later in the article he says:

One can often be in doubt about the effect of a word or a phrase, and one needs rules that one can rely on when instinct fails. I think the following rules will cover most cases:

1. Never use a metaphor, simile, or other figure of speech which you are used to seeing in print.
2. Never use a long word where a short one will do.
3. If it is possible to cut a word out, always cut it out.
4. Never use the passive where you can use the active.
5. Never use a foreign phrase, a scientific word, or a jargon word if you can think of an everyday English equivalent.
6. Break any of these rules sooner than say anything outright barbarous.

6 | Teams and joint bids

Teamwork

We have looked at some of the processes involved in developing a proposal, both before anyone starts to write, and at each stage involving a written document or accompanying letter.

Almost everything so far has been applicable to individuals or groups. Once a group increases to five or more people, you start to need systems for knowledge-sharing and definition of individual roles within the joint venture. You need a project manager (sometimes called a project contractor) and back-up administration. And since groups can easily misunderstand each other or divide into factions, it is sensible to decide who is responsible for what. This could include (but is not limited to):

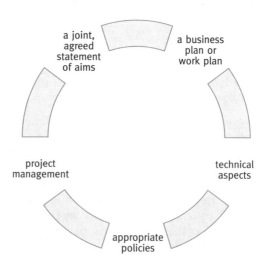

a joint, agreed statement of aims

a business plan or work plan

project management

technical aspects

appropriate policies

Role-play

In addition to defining individual roles within a project, it can be useful for teams to bounce ideas off each other. On pages 25–6, we talked about looking at all aspects of a project proposal. A further idea—suitable for team bids—is to role-play. This applies to responses to an invitation to tender from a client requesting bids for work (not for a public grant).

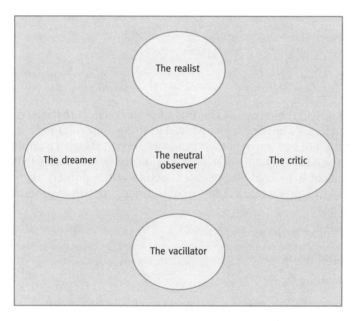

Assess your client team and give them personalities like the ones in the diagram. Each member of your team 'plays' one of these roles in turn. As the 'dreamer' they think up the most creative brief regardless of cost. As the 'critic' they knock down every suggestion.

Let each team member represent a role in turn and imagine what each 'client' may be looking for from you. In between each role-play, return to the 'neutral observer' to put the voice of reason. This helps everyone get into the mind of the client and anticipate their questions.

This exercise can take place at the planning stage and is most useful when your team is going to meet 'their' team.

Project management

Project management is particularly important where there are several partners in the project. Many government-funded, and all European Union, projects involve consortia with a lead partner managing the whole project. The 'Partnerships with People' philosophy highlights five key themes of management practice:

Shared effort

Shared goals

Shared culture

Management practice

Shared learning

Shared information

It is outside the scope of this book to steer readers through the minefield of bureaucracy involved in these huge joint bids: it is enough to be aware that winning large contracts with complex partnerships is an art in itself. Our concern here is with smaller teams of five to ten individuals. A good starting point is to break the project tasks into small components. These generally include:

- project management;
- administration;
- mailing lists;
- research (e.g. surveys, action research, questionnaire analysis, interviews);
- report writing;
- financial procedures;
- promotion and dissemination;
- evaluation.

In a large organization, there would be a department responsible for each task. The project manager will be in overall control of making sure everyone works together and will probably be the one who puts together the initial proposal—with the collaboration of all partners. That person must be prepared to edit all contributions so they have a homogeneity and read as if they are written by the same hand.

The business plan

Chapter 4 suggested various additional documents that you might offer and one of these is a business plan.

Small companies benefit from a business plan—if only because the very act of focusing on a long-term idea of where you want to be in three to five years' time helps to crystallize thoughts and identify priorities. That is true of individuals as well, though whether your plan is a growing tick-list or a more extended document depends on how organized you are.

A new year's resolution is a form of business plan.

If you are looking for funding, it is worth writing one simply as a 'sales' exercise. It will demonstrate confidence in yourself or your group and that will help your cause. Besides, someone might ask for it. So even if the plan begins life for personal use, write it as if it is for an outsider.

Content of a plan

Base the plan on detailed information where possible. But do not include all the detail in the plan. Keep it short.

- Focus on what the reader needs to know.

- Describe briefly (without padding) what you do.

- Say what you hope to achieve, and by when.

- Decide on half a dozen objectives and define clear targets for these; then think about how you will achieve these and work towards them.

- Say what is special about your group, where it fits in the market, who its competitors are, and how that impacts on you.

- Say through what channels you reach your audience or users (e.g. media coverage, advertisements, mail order, etc.) and how you plan to increase that.

- Include some financial information (a full budget in the case of a large project). Remember to check that the figures are the same as any you gave in costings at the application package stage (see page 55).

■ Analyse how committed all the people in the team are and what further ways of motivating them there are.

■ Put any substantial information (e.g. market research, group literature, CVs, etc.) in an appendix.

Detailed business plans age fast, so it is best to stick to overall principles. Have a six-month short-term plan for the immediate shopping list.

Obviously, the larger the business is, the more complex the business plan. A craftsman or a small dance company, say, will not expect to analyse its management information systems, but that might be a key exercise for a business focusing on product sales. Comparing efficiency ratios with competitors is useful for anyone (even a writer) and most people do this, even though they may not formalize it as part of a business plan.

Joint bids

There are countless research projects involving small teams who put together a joint bid. Many originate in higher education institutions; others in industry; others in self-formed groups. On the whole, they fall outside the scope of this book because we are concentrating here on groups with modest projects in mind. Nevertheless, it is useful for individuals to know a little about the procedures.

Government is either organized benevolence or organized madness; its peculiar magnitude permits no shading.

John Updike

Government

Projects of all hues in the UK are funded by government departments or quangos (such as the British Council). Funding opportunities are generally announced in appropriate 'trade' journals, the national or scientific press (e.g. the *New Scientist*) and on the departmental web site. Advertisements tend to give quite short deadlines, allowing maybe two weeks to two months to prepare a proposal. So it is better to monitor the department's web site for details of forthcoming tenders (and the guidelines that go with them). New initiatives tend to be announced between January and May.

The tendering process for government research grants usually takes the form of an invitation to submit an expression of interest or outline proposal. The department will then invite short-listed applicants to submit a full bid. These are assessed by an evaluation panel and/or external reviewers, and the contract awarded on the basis of quality, cost, and the expertise of the proposers.

European Union (EU)

Applying for grants or funding under the various EU initiatives works according to rigid and inflexible rules and is not for the faint-hearted. There will normally be a call for proposals. It will be carefully worded so as to preclude a flood of applications likely to be rejected subsequently and you must get all the details and read them in depth.

EU-funded projects are a law unto themselves. There is no point in trying to write a project around the EU programme criteria, but if the criteria match something that you are already doing, and offer the chance to diversify, innovate, or reach different markets, and there is real opportunity for a European dimension, then it might be for you.

Before you start writing a proposal, look at:

■ information available on the appropriate EU web sites;

■ the call for proposals in the official Journal;

■ programme application packs and Vademecum;

■ directories on previous projects that have been funded under the programme (if available).

See also the checklists in Part B, pages 124–5.

Having decided to continue, make a list of the key words from the documentation and note the core programme objectives. Check the eligibility criteria—focus of the funding, number of partners, types of partners—and make sure you qualify. Check the deadline for pre-proposals and proposals.

Managing teams of writers

Part of the project manager's responsibilities will be to edit materials coming from different members of the team—in some cases from different countries. This requires skill and diplomacy.

Boilerplating

A short-cut to aid team writing is 'boilerplating': reusing paragraphs of standard text or graphics. In a large development project maintained by teams of authors, there will almost certainly be interrelated sections and reusable parts. The teams who are best at producing winning proposals are able to make intelligent use of such boilerplate materials.

They must be maintained in some form that allows convenient

■ cataloguing

■ updating

■ retrieval.

So you will probably need a sophisticated software system. If this is not available to you, then you could consider creating a template for use by all members of the team.

Using standard paragraphs can be a tremendous time saver if used judiciously. But do be very careful. It is all too easy to block-copy details that apply to one project without removing the tell-tale signs that they do not apply to the current one. Careless use of boilerplate sections could imply that you will serve the client in an equally careless manner. So always read through everything with great care.

Profiling the team members

It is always a good idea to profile the members of your team to establish credentials. This is usually best placed as one of the

Appendices to the presentation document. (I have put my own at the back of this book, page 134.)

Whether you decide to do this with 100-word mini-profiles or with full-blown CVs depends on the project and on the requirements. A nice touch, if budget or expertise allow, is to include small portrait photographs of the team.

It does look more professional if you standardize all the contributions your colleagues send you. This will also make you look like a team, rather than a bunch of individuals. In other words, even CVs need editing—and it might mean ruthless cutting. If it does, explain to your colleague why you are doing so.

For example, if one member has included a publications list, performance list (or other similar), but the others haven't, either omit it or ask others to do the same. You could keep the list more manageable by citing only the most recent three or five. Similarly, consider how many past jobs or educational qualifications to include and do the same for everyone.

You could design a form like the one below and ask colleagues to complete it, rather than adapting their standard CVs.

Name	
Job title	
Project role and objectives	*State in about 50 words what you bring to the project*
Experience	*In no more than 50 words, say what background knowledge you bring to the project. Then list (in bullet-point form) the last 3 relevant jobs you have done in this area.*
Qualifications	*Include higher education or professional qualifications only*
Memberships	*Society or club memberships can show calibre and may appeal to those with similar interests*
Other	*Professional achievements (e.g. publications, CDs, etc.)*

Project approval

Many joint proposals are subject to an internal approval process rather than geared towards outside funding. The principles are the same. The champion of a particular project has to prove to others in the company that the project is viable.

It is useful to have guidelines to suggest ways in which your team might measure new opportunities and the procedures by which these are presented.

On page 96 are some guiding principles that should act as a safety-valve in assessing risk—but for each organization the checklist will need to be tailored. Use them as a starting point upon which to base the procedure that is right for you.

All projects will go through an internal approval process, which each group can formalize by naming the individuals or departments that must approve the proposal at each stage. You might decide on some approval stages such as these:

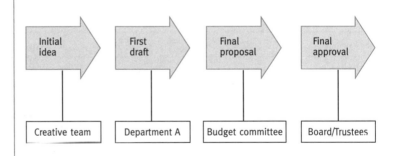

To sum up . . .

The more people you get in a group working together, the more you need to define responsibilities and agree standards. So if you are one of a team, you can expect:

1. to have a role within the organization, either as the project manager or working for that person;

2. to co-operate with your colleagues and contribute ideas;

3. to participate in team-building exercises as required;

4. to offer ideas for a business plan;

5. to monitor complex requirements in a large joint bid;

6. your written work to be edited to conform to a house style;

7. to agree policies and participate in any project approval mechanism.

Participate in team-building exercises as required.

7 Continuing partnerships

*Major
areas of
government
support:*

- innovation and technology
- business support
- community development
- health
- education, training, and culture

See Part B, pages
125ff., for further
detail on applying
for government
funding.

In chapter 3, we touched on the importance of developing a partnership as you put together the elements of the initial proposal. It is vital to keep lines of communication open all through the project—and after it has finished.

There is no magic formula for identifying what makes partnerships work. Sometimes it is simply a matter of good group dynamics. It is not easy to change that, but the more aware you are of what partners expect from you, the easier it will be for personal and group relationships to flourish. Ask yourself—at various stages of the joint endeavour:

- What am I bringing to the project?
- What am I getting out of it?
- Are others supportive, neutral, or hostile?
- How can I involve or motivate other people?

Working in partnership

The current view of all funding bodies—banks, venture capitalists, business angels, government, charities, foundations—is that you and they are entering a partnership. There must be something in it for them. Sometimes, it is a partnership of profit on both sides. The bank lends you money to kick-start an idea, and takes a share of the profits as they roll in. Usually it is much more subtle than that, as the case history on page 27 shows. It is quite rarely pure altruistic charity.

Everyone is looking for the 'win-win' alliance. That should be the first thing you think of.

The government has a wide-ranging programme of grants. The partnership pay-off is that they will get a more efficient and productive work force as a result. And loyal to the funding party too. The Small Business Service (which confusingly retains its old acronym SMART) is one that helps individuals, and small and medium-sized businesses to develop technologically innovative products and processes. It is typical in that it offers bursaries from a few thousand pounds to £150,000 (Euro 240,000) and it has the catch that all government grants have: the amount of paperwork is huge. You probably need a finance director who can spend a week on it all. Something you will not have, or you would not be buying this book.

If you are a bit of an entrepreneur, then the chances are paperwork isn't your forte. So think quite carefully before you embark on a partnership that is going to make demands on you that you will find difficult to meet. It needs to be right for both sides of the partnership.

There is little doubt that gaining sponsorship or funding is much harder for individuals. Large companies are seeking to cut down on administrative costs and it is more cost-effective to give larger grants to high-profile activities or events than a few hundred to a small individual. So look for companies that have decentralized giving policies. For example, Barclays Bank gives its 35 head offices discretionary limits to spend on local communities.

Seek out other companies that do the same. This will not be easy because listings of companies supporting individuals are hard to find. The Hollis directory, for example (see Part B, page 131) lists several hundred companies supporting a wide range of activities in education and media, and only six of those say they support individuals. This is approximately 1% of the total number of companies offering funding.

Sponsorship can play a significant role in a downturn because it performs various marketing tasks.

Alastair Ritchie,
Octagon Sports Marketing
Consultancy

Termination

Partnerships can go wrong. One early task is to anticipate all the ways in which the partnership's success could be threatened because it is important to make provision for that in the construction of the proposal. It is good project management to consider your exit strategy at any point.

Everyone should know how long the partnership is intended to last; and whether an extension might be negotiated if, after joint evaluation, both parties agree the relationship has succeeded and want to continue.

Or, if your organization is involved in a joint project that flounders for some reason, you would want to decide:

■ who owns the intellectual property of what remains of the joint venture;

■ who owns any equipment;

■ whether any funds have to be returned or reallocated;

and other equally knotty problems. It is better to think these things through before they happen so that you have agreements in place in case relationships turn sour.

Risk analysis

What risks are there in the project and what might prevent it being successful? For example, the foot-and-mouth epidemic in the UK in 2001 meant cancellation of many outdoor and indoor events, many of which were to take place as the result of a successful bidding process. This is called 'force majeure' and is something no one can predict and so cannot protect themselves from. Riots, industrial action, and floods are other examples of 'force majeure'.

It is advisable to have a clause for this in your formal agreement. For example, request that the contract can be terminated without either party being held liable, except maybe for a part refund of the agreed fee (depending on the circumstances). You should make sure that you will not be accountable for repayment of any fees from which the funder has clearly benefited—advertising or media exposure, for example.

What's in it for the funder

A bit of funding jargon is 'Lead with the need.' That doesn't mean your need, but why they need what you have to give. Most businesses are increasingly aware that much of what they do has a positive or negative effect on how they are perceived by their employees and by the outside world. They welcome associations that put them in a positive light. So however you choose to present your case, make sure it spells out why the funder's reputation will benefit. Remember that community involvement is a nebulous term and different companies may have different names for it. For example:

Did you know?
Sports sponsorship attracts 90% of all UK recreation funding.

- corporate community involvement (CCI);

- community affairs;

- community partnerships;

- corporate social responsibility (CSR).

It helps to know a bit more about the things that businesses will fund. On page 25 there is a chart showing what industry sectors are looking for in partnerships and what they expect from them.

Acknowledgements

A small point, but one that is often forgotten—always acknowledge the source of external support in all documentation. This will generally be part of the deal, but some grants are given without any strings attached. If so, the funder will nevertheless notice and appreciate it if you mention their name wherever possible—especially in circumstances where they least expect it.

When companies put something tangible into the community, it's very good for their corporate pride and employees' morale. It's also healthy for their reputation because pressure is increasing for companies to be seen to be contributing to society rather than simply making donations behind the scenes.

Heart of the City

Fulfilling the targets

Maintaining confidence

Keep in touch with the right person. Identify and agree at the first meeting how you will communicate. Options include:

Method of communication	Advantages	Disadvantages
Email	Immediate Cheap Encourages prompt response Keeps everyone informed May be filed and used in audits	Unstable standards for sending or receiving attachments Can be ambiguous or blunt Anxieties about viruses Growth of junk mail
Telephone (including mobiles)	Personal Immediate reply Creative chat	Expensive Frequency of answerphone
Telephone conferencing	Useful to discuss a specific issue Effective when well-chaired	Ineffective for general discussion
Video-conferencing	Saves on travel time Partners have a visual image	Expensive Unreliable Access still restricted
Fax	May be personalized Good for sketches Record available	Lack of confidentiality in open offices May be distorted on arrival
Computer conferencing software	Efficient filing of all relevant work On-going discussion possible	Relies on partners going into the conference/bulletin board
Face-to-face	Best way to resolve major problems and build on trust Indicates concern and support	Expensive in travel costs and time

Progress reports

A weakness of many bids is a lack of foresight in considering how to evaluate and monitor them. You may decide to do this internally. If so, agree with the client or funder how you will do this at the outset. A useful starting point is to ask all involved to complete a short evaluation form after key meetings. It is also worth seeing if there is anything in the budget for an external evaluator who can take an objective approach.

An evaluator might ask questions like:

- How was the project successful/not so successful?
- Is it worth continuing or imitating elsewhere?
- What is the impact of the project?
- Are there opportunities to transfer experiences to future projects?
- Where will the partnership/products go next?

Both the project process and any products (including performance or sports events) can be evaluated. An evaluator will collect quantitative and qualitative data to support the process. This may mean working in groups, supporting interviews, or completing questionnaires.

Whether you opt for an internal or external evaluation process, remember that the proposal on which it is based needs to highlight the aims, objectives, targets, and goals. Otherwise, there is nothing to focus on for the evaluation.

To sum up . . .

A current popular buzz phrase for successful partnerships is 'win-win', or for those who do not want competitive images, 'gain-gain'. That means developing long-term partnerships with businesses to bring positive benefits to everyone involved. The business gains from an enhanced image and community respect through its involvement with you: you gain funding, exchange of expertise, mentoring, or payment in kind. Bear in mind that:

1. There is giving and receiving on both sides.
2. Sponsors have needs too. Always acknowledge your partners.
3. You may succeed if you find out as much as you can about your partners, and assess any risks.
4. Make sure you communicate at all stages.
5. Give partners frequent progress reports so they always know if you are on target for your plan or if anything requires replanning.

Part B: Reference Section
Contents

Sample guidelines and checklists

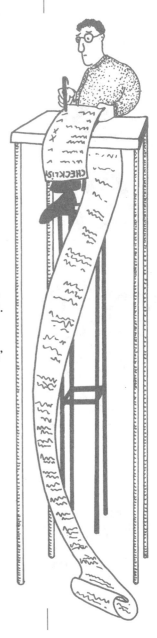

Part A concentrates on general principles. It also acknowledges that each reader of this book is coming with a specific area of interest in mind. Many will be individuals looking for sponsorship and others are working in larger groups piecing together bids for work. As Part A shows, the differences are mainly in the detail.

Part B looks at the detail and gives specimen documents, guidelines, and categorized sources of other information.

The ideas and checklists offered in this section are not a guarantee for success; however, they do offer useful 'tips' (all of which have been discussed in more detail in Part A).

Approaches to a brief

The brief will depend on the outcome it intends to generate. In responding to a brief, you may find it helpful to check whether it is important to think about it as a description of a process or a requirement for an outcome, because your bid will vary in its style accordingly.

See 'The brief' in Part A, pages 31–2.

specifying process

The grass will be cut every two weeks.

specifying outcome

The grass will be no higher than 40 mm.

Process specifications

This defines every activity, standard, labour, capital, and materials, together with the method of delivery.

Advantage	Disadvantage
Very specific Easy to evaluate Cost easily fixed You know what you have to supply and how to deliver it Easier to define, therefore gives fewer risks, provided the description is clear and comprehensive	May not allow for improvements.to service or equipment, or changing needs The bidder has no flexibility to innovate and improve If it is not specified precisely, there is little scope to argue for inclusion of unspecified or insufficiently specified needs

Outcome specifications

This concentrates on the actual outcome, i.e. the end result, the time for achievement, and the intended effect.

Advantage	Disadvantage
Gives the bidder more freedom,which could lead to improvements Allows introduction of new working methods Says what should be delivered without specifying how it should be done	Hard to determine what is the best method at the best price at any time Success depends on the ability to specify the outcome clearly May be hard to compare offers

Method checklist

If you concentrate on outcomes then you, as the bidder, must provide written details of exactly how you would organize and develop the services that will lead to the result.

These written details form the method statements and demonstrate the level of understanding and knowledge you have of the tasks required by the specification. Use the tick boxes to check whether you have defined:

- ☑ a method of working;
- ☑ how you intend to deliver the contract;
- ☑ a timescale with review points;
- ☑ how the programme will be resourced;
- ☑ how you (and therefore the client) might measure quality;
- ☑ policies, e.g. environmental, energy efficiency, health and safety, training, or project management methodology;
- ☑ proposed sub-contractors, if allowed;
- ☑ transitional or start-up arrangements;
- ☑ training needs;
- ☑ proposals for continuous improvement.

When these method statements are evaluated they provide information about your:

- ■ ability to provide the service;
- ■ understanding of the service;
- ■ awareness of the client's requirements;
- ■ level of originality;
- ■ organization.

I/We undertake to:
1. Draft, edit, advise, and otherwise contribute to the production of XYZ.
2. Prepare position papers for internal and external meetings.
3. Contribute to the evaluation, monitoring, and review of XYZ.
4. Liaise with partner organizations, including employers, professional bodies, and with the client, as required.
5. Set up, organize, and run workshops as agreed.
6. Produce quarterly reports (or as required).

Proposals for the arts checklist

Arts sponsorship is far harder to get than support for sports. So woolly thinking is unlikely to attract funding. You have to work quite hard to anticipate and answer any queries an arts sponsor might have. Pre-empt these by answering the questions below.

What is it?

☐ details of art work/event/performance, etc.

☐ venue

☐ date and time

☐ who else is involved

What are the aims?

☐ why you want to do it

☐ what the audience is

☐ who benefits

☐ how it relates to your other work

☐ outcomes of the project

☐ how it might continue after this occasion

How will the practicalities be resolved?

☐ medium used and design implications

☐ costs

☐ how people who will be affected will be consulted

☐ supporting evidence from people involved

What resources are required?

☐ space

☐ materials and equipment

☐ transport

☐ insurance

☐ health and safety issues

☐ timescales

Who are you?

☐ CVs

Proposals for sports: model letter

The following letter is adapted (with permission) from one suggested by the Sports Sponsorship Advisory Service.

Dear [Named Person],
Re: Sponsorship of XYZ sporting organisation

Would your organization be interested in sponsoring our Junior team? We are one of the leading sports clubs in the region and are known for excellence (see the attached brochure). The Junior team is a new venture. It has already made a significant national impact. We anticipate that it will be in the top ten at next year's British Championships.

I am writing to you because your product has direct appeal for our players and spectators. So sponsorship of the Junior team would raise your profile to a potential audience of over 5,000 customers. In return for your investment in the team we offer you the following benefits:

- Branding on all kit and equipment;
- Direct exposure to 200 participants and 1,000 spectators at the Championships;
- 2 minutes' coverage on Sky Sports 3 with an audience of 2,000;
- 10 column inches in the national press, often with specific reference to sponsors;
- Several feature articles in the regional press;
- Branded column in our newsletter—circulation 1,000 (the media predictions are best estimates based on past experience).

We believe these benefits, coupled with the positive association between our organizations, is worth about £5,000. That said, we are very flexible and can tailor any sponsorship to your marketing needs.

Thank you for taking the time to read this letter. If I may, I will phone your office in the next few days to arrange a convenient time to discuss the details of this proposed partnership.

Yours sincerely,

Sponsorship Co-ordinator

Proposals for training guidelines

The Charities Aid Foundation (CAF) fast track fund is targeted
at organizations seeking funding for specific training needs. Its
guidelines (reproduced below by kind permission of the CAF)
form a useful model.

Fast track fund

Investing in training is essential for any organization that
wishes to develop or expand. We want to support organizations
seeking immediate funding for specific training needs.

The focus of this training must be on strengthening your
organization.

Funding priorities

We will give priority to training that aims to strengthen your
organization's structure. We will fund training for financial
management, fund-raising, or governance issues. This could
include training for staff, volunteers, or Management
Committee members.

Priority is given to immediate training needs. You will need to
have identified the training course and/or training agency.

What will we fund?

Training costs to attend specified courses.

Costs to cover training provided by a consultant.

What we will not fund

This fund is for training costs only. We will not fund any other
costs.

Spending that has already taken place.

Who can apply?

Applications will be considered from:

- Any organization in the UK which is set up for exclusively charitable purposes.

- Organizations with an annual income of up to £1,500,000.

- However, priority for 100% funding will be given to organizations with an income of £50,000 or less per year. We will assess your financial position when prioritizing applications.

How much will we give?

Up to £600.

When to apply?

There are no deadlines. You can apply throughout the year. We will let you know if you have been awarded a grant within 10 working days. If any information is missing we will need to get back to you and this will delay our decision.

Source: <http://www.cafonline.org/grants/g_ftfund.cfm>

Pre-proposal form

On the next page is a sample form for a mini-project (which can be adapted for training or start-up funding. You would be expected to complete it in conjunction with the notes for applicants (assuming there are some). These should give relevant criteria to help you complete the sections below. Follow any word count given (if it *is* given), bearing in mind that no section should be longer than 500 words.

Title of proposal:	
Name of proposer(s):	
Institution/group name:	
Address:	
Phone:	
Fax:	
Email:	

Provide a brief description of your project (about 100 words). If your bid is successful this will be used to announce the project.

Total funding requested:	
Relevance of the project:	
Potential benefit to the funding community:	
Dissemination plans:	
How will you evaluate the effectiveness of your project?	
Outline the proposed timetable for the work with milestones.	
Give details of the costs involved (your time and other costs). How does the project provide value for money?	
Signature of proposer:	
Signature of referee:	

Sponsorship profiling template

The template that follows is adapted from the registration form at the online community for matching individuals and organizations with business opportunities, at <http://www.sponsorshiponline.com/>. It is a useful exercise for fund-seekers to fill it in.

Company/organization name   Phone
Contact name   Fax
Address   Email

1. Please enter the title of your project . . . .

   Sponsorship categories (please highlight one)

   ☐ Sport & entertainment

   ☐ Business

   ☐ Social & community

   ☐ Arts & media

   ☐ Other

   Sponsorship details (please highlight one)

   ☐ Individual

   ☐ Team/club

   ☐ Organization

   ☐ One off event/production

   ☐ Other

2. Is this a new or existing event/activity?

   ☐ New

   ☐ Existing

3. Sponsorship location

   ☐ UK

   ☐ European

---

4. Key audiences you will reach (please indicate relevant groups)

Gender

☐ Male

☐ Female

☐ Both

Age

☐ Under 10

☐ 10–15

☐ 15–25

☐ 25–34

☐ 45 plus

5. Please give a short description (30 words) of the opportunity, which will be used as a headline and be seen by all potential sponsors.

Please give a more detailed (100 word) description, which will be seen by sponsors who are specifically interested in what you can offer.

6. What sort of sponsorship are you looking for?

☐ Title

☐ Principal sponsor

☐ Official supplier

☐ General association

☐ Personal sponsor

☐ Other (please detail)

7. Media coverage location

☐ UK

☐ Multi-country

☐ European

Please explain what type of media coverage you will receive in the areas selected in no more than 50 words. Please list any other opportunities for brand awareness, e.g. advertising banners, programmes, leaflets, etc. in no more than 50 words.

If the sponsorship will drive traffic to a sponsor's web site please tick the ways in which this will be achieved below:

- ☐ web site links;
- ☐ advertising;
- ☐ access to membership database;
- ☐ publicity on printed materials;
- ☐ other (please detail below).

8. If the sponsorship will showcase the sponsor's product or service please explain how in no more than 50 words.

   If corporate hospitality is possible please explain how in no more than 50 words.

   If you will be able to provide your sponsors with access to a database please explain how in less than 50 words.

   List any other benefits not included above (50 words max).

   Dates and duration of events (50 words max).

9. Please give details of current or historic sponsors (50 words max).

10. Why should a sponsor consider this opportunity? An opportunity for you to explain why a sponsor should investigate this opportunity further (100 words max).

11. How much are you looking for?
    - ☐ £0–20,000
    - ☐ £20–50,000
    - ☐ £50–100,000
    - ☐ £100,000–250,000
    - ☐ Over £250,000

    Please specify the exact amount you require.

    What are the costs of individual opportunities? Please list if relevant.

Project development guidelines

Principles

All potential projects should be in tune with the aims of the team/group/organization, which are to:

■ [Your mission statement or aims]

Definition of project

A project is defined as any significant change or development whose successful implementation depends upon the investment of new resources (cash or people).

Process

Many projects will go through a number of stages and it is important for everyone to be aware of where they are in this process. The stages would probably involve:

■ ideas generation and discussion;

■ discussion of outline ideas with the appropriate committee, focusing on the value of the idea and not on the specifics of the business;

■ budgetary considerations;

■ appointment a project manager and team who will decide whether the project is viable;

■ approval by the relevant committee/Board/Trustees.

The project manager should indicate how the decision-making process will develop, with some indication of timescale (though this can be imprecise in the early stages).

Documents should always have an executive summary of not more than one page giving the main points of information and argument in the paper.

The proposal should contain:

☐ clear details about the objectives of the study or project;

☐ how you intend to develop the idea;

☐ the benefits to the group, community, or organization;

☐ how the objectives of the project or study will be realized;

☐ a schedule of milestones and deadlines of the intended outcomes and deliverables;

☐ project management details (may not apply to individuals);

☐ a dissemination strategy;

☐ an indication of the skills and expertise of the applicant or team, clearly indicating the particular qualities and relevant experience that they will bring to the project;

☐ a summary of anticipated costs, including a rough indication of the breakdown of this cost;

☐ discussion of risks and consequences.

Sealed bids

Sealed bids normally apply to publicly advertised projects and are usually opened in public on a set date. If there are no guidelines, you can include a cover sheet like this one (and include some details on the footer of each page).

Name & address	Signature of person authorized to sign	Your bid £	Bid no.
	Telephone		
	Fax	Date of your bid	
	Email		

This bid is firm 30 days from date of opening unless otherwise noted.

The successful bidder guarantees delivery within ____ days after receipt of order at address shown.

Finance

Events that may be held for fund-raising without attracting tax (no more than 15 in a year):

- A ball, dinner dance, disco, or barn dance.
- A performance such as a concert, stage production, and any other event which has a paying audience.
- The showing of a film.
- A fête, fair or festival, auction, or horticultural show.
- An exhibition such as art, history, or science.
- A bazaar, jumble sale, car boot sale, or a good-as-new sale.
- A sporting performance or sporting participation (including spectators), such as a sponsored walk or swim.
- A game of skill, a contest, or a quiz.
- Participation in an endurance event.
- A fireworks display.
- A dinner, lunch, or barbecue.

See also pages 46 ff. in Part A.

Tax

Tax law changes frequently so it is always advisable to have the latest information from an accountant in your country of residence. There is extensive up-to-date information about UK tax on the Inland Revenue web site <http://www.inlandrevenue.gov.uk/> and the Customs & Excise web site <http://www.hmce.gov.uk/>.

Some things to find out are:

☐ whether a received grant, donation, or sponsorship sum is tax free or not;

☐ whether the donor can set gifts against corporation tax:

- the answer will probably be yes, if it is wholly and exclusively for the purpose of trade

- if it is revenue and not capital expenditure

- entertaining clients will not normally be tax-deductible; however charity events are exempt from income tax and corporation tax as long as the profits are applied charitably (see box);

☐ whether membership or friends schemes are treated in the same way as cash donations;

☐ whether a loan is tax free and what the interest repayment situation is;

☐ how to evaluate and declare sponsorship in kind to the tax authorities: giving company products to an organization may be treated in the same way as giving cash;

- what tax arrangements apply for artists or writers in residence;
- whether payroll gifting is a possibility;
- how Gift Aid can work to your advantage;
- how to claim back tax;
- what the VAT implications are.

Invoice summary note

If you invoice for the work in stages, it is useful for the project manager to track progress during the course of the project. Here is a sample form which can be signed by the client and the manager as a way of agreeing what stage the project has reached:

Project title:

Project manager: Email:

Contract no.:   Contracted period:

Invoice no. and date: Amount: £

Outcomes for period of invoice:

Summary of work completed:

Issues/problems to be noted:

Comments:

Signed: . . . .

Date: . . . .

                                     (Project manager)

Approved by client: Yes   /   No

Comments:

Signed: . . . .

Date: . . . .

                                     (Client)

Terms and conditions

It is unlikely that you will need to write a set of terms and conditions as they must always be couched in the appropriate legal language. But it *is* a good idea to think about what you are committing yourself to, and to look out for points such as these:

Acceptance or rejection of bids, proposals, or funding applications: (e.g. whether the funder reserves the right to accept or reject.)

Assignment, transfer, and subcontracting: (e.g. under what circumstances you can get others to do part of the work.)

Compliance with laws: (e.g. liability, access, and so on.)

Compliance with scope of work: (e.g. precisely what specifications describe the properties or materials, the dimensions, quality, reliability level, quantities, delivery schedules, or other characteristics and requirements with which you must comply.)

Conformance with contract: (e.g. whether alteration of the terms, conditions, delivery, price, quality, quantities, or specifications of this contract can be granted without prior written consent.)

Facsimile or email responses: (e.g. whether these are admissible or whether signatures are required.)

Failure to honour bid/proposal: (e.g. procedures if the work is not done or is not satisfactory.)

Indemnification: (e.g. what happens if there is negligence on either side.)

Intellectual property: (e.g. who owns what at the end of the project.)

Late bids and proposals: (e.g. whether late bids and proposals will automatically be disqualified.)

Payment term: (e.g. 30 days to pay invoices and whether there are milestones for parts of the project.)

Termination of contract: (e.g. circumstances in which the contract can be terminated.)

Protest procedure: (e.g. what happens in cases of dispute.)

Online advice

There is a great deal of online advice for people seeking funding. This listing is representative of places to go beyond the scope of this book for further detailed advice in various sectors. There are many more, as you will find if you type some keywords associated with your own quest into a search engine. Try to refine the keywords to avoid thousands of hits. E.g.:

sponsorship + jazz
fund-raising + children

You can telephone to request information from some sites below if you do not have web access. They are unlikely, however, to be able to answer specific queries about where to go for money.

BDS Sponsorship web site

European resource centre for sponsors and those seeking sponsorship, offering knowledge consultancy, reference texts, and databases.

Web site: <http://www.sponsorship.co.uk/>
Tel: 020 7689 3333

CharityNet

A global online resource which brings together the web sites of non-profit organizations across the world. Free registration.

Web site: <http://www.charitynet.org/>
No telephone number on site.

FunderFinder

Small national (UK) charity that produces software for grant-seekers: try its excellent free software 'Apply Yourselves', whose advice cannot be bettered (indeed acknowledgement for some ideas in this book must be made to it).

Professional consultancy services offer:

- sponsorship and allied income generation strategy
- feasibility studies
- evaluation
- competitive analysis
- evaluation and pricing
- integrated marketing programmes

Web site: <http://www.funderfinder.org.uk/>
Tel: 0113 243 3008

FunderFinder PIN (People In Need)

This is a software package which will help identify unusual charitable trusts and foundations nationally. It appears to pitch at educational development, but the remit is very wide so it is worth looking at for any developmental funding. An application form to help identify your own unique specialisms or needs is available.

Web site: <http://www.learning-matters.co.uk/>
Tel: 0800 515547

Fund-raising UK

Consultancy in Internet fund-raising offering free advice (and paid-for courses). See its bookshop categories on page 130 for specialist literature.

Web site: <http://www.fundraising.co.uk/>
Tel: 020 8640 5233

Grants On-Line

Invaluable subscriptions service offering:

- Access to information on the latest and current calls for proposals.
- Access to a comprehensive online Grant Directory covering European Union, UK Government, National Lottery, New Opportunities Fund, and UK Grant Making Trusts.
- Automatic subscription to a fortnightly External Funding Alert.
- Sliding scale of subscription rates. There is a 14–day free trial of great benefit to individuals.

Web site: <http://www.grantsonline.org.uk/>
Tel: 01202 828674

Homeworking

Home-spun site offering information and support to those working from home. Includes some advice on how to write a business plan.

Web site: <http://www.homeworking.com/>
Fax: 0870 284 8769

Institute of Fund-raising

Aimed at charities, but some useful gleanings for the individual. See its Codes of Fund-raising Practice to outline best practice across the full range of fund-raising activities.

Web site: <http://www.icfm.org.uk/>
Tel: 020 7627 3436

Legacy Promotion Campaign

Tries to encourage people to make tax-efficient donations in their wills and to raise charity awareness in businesses.

Web site: <http://www.legacypromotioncampaign.org.uk/>
Tel: 020 7930 3154

Sponsorship Online

An international database that aims to be an online marketplace where sponsors and sponsorship seekers can find each other. There is a registration fee for people in search of sponsorship and a registration form similar in substance to the profile template on pages 109–111.

Web site: <http://www.sponsorshiponline.com/>
Tel: 01428 751195

Sports Sponsorship Advisory Service

As the site says, 'Perseverance is likely to be the key'. The service aims: 'To better equip sport and recreation to gain and develop commercial sponsorship'.

Web site: <http://www.sponsorship-advice.org/>
Tel: 020 7854 8599

TED Tenders Electronic Daily

Official Journal of the European Community: has to publish information about the majority of public sector contracts and tenders in Europe. It is comprehensive, but also very complex.

Web site: <http://ted.eur-op.eu.int>
No telephone number on site.

UK Sponsorship database

Thousands of current sponsorship opportunities and jobs. Ongoing sponsorships in a variety of categories.

Web site: <http://www.uksponsorship.com/>
Tel: 01487 815395

Major funding bodies

The information in this section focuses mainly on funding opportunities in the UK and Europe.

EU

Details of how to go about applying for EU grants or funding are on page 89. Calls for proposals will set out the following information:

- the context;
- the subject of the call for proposals;
- the total budget available for the programme;
- the likely number of beneficiaries (and hence the average amount of any grant);
- regulations for partnerships;
- the scale of Commission participation in percentage terms;
- whether or not contributions in kind are taken into account when calculating the grant;
- the maximum amount of any grant;
- the rules governing which organizations and operations are eligible for assistance;
- the selection criteria for operations;
- the rules governing which categories of expenditure are eligible and which are not;
- the rules for judging evaluation, monitoring, and controls (technical and financial);

- the deadlines applicable;
- general arrangements for submitting applications for grants.

(Detail taken from the EU Vademecum on Grant Management for applicants and beneficiaries, 48pp, available online at <http://europa.eu.int/comm/secretariat_general/sgc/info_subv/vm_gm.htm> [accessed 20 August 2003].)

Identifying potential partners

Project partners should recognize that they need:

☐ a common philosophy and approach to activities;

☐ written clarification of the purposes of the project;

☐ agreement on transnational activities;

☐ a similar range and level of activities, professional knowledge, and experience;

☐ an interest in learning new skills and meeting challenges;

☐ an involvement in promoting and encouraging European integration and knowledge of other cultures;

☐ realistic and innovative attitudes to transnational partnerships and co-operation;

☐ a clear idea of how to put partnership into practice;

☐ opportunity and commitment to financially resource projects (including matched funding);

☐ common working language(s) at meetings and in documentation;

☐ commitment at senior management level;

☐ defined roles and responsibilities of the individuals involved.

The diagram overleaf gives you some idea of the vast number of EU grants there are—each with its own binding rules and criteria. (Courtesy of <http://www.grantsonline.org.uk/>, which also lists UK Government Grants, National Lottery Grants, Scottish Grants, and Welsh Grants.)

Tip
If you are bidding for European Social Fund (ESF) grants, you may need expert guidance on how to fill in grants applications and what those assessing them are looking for.

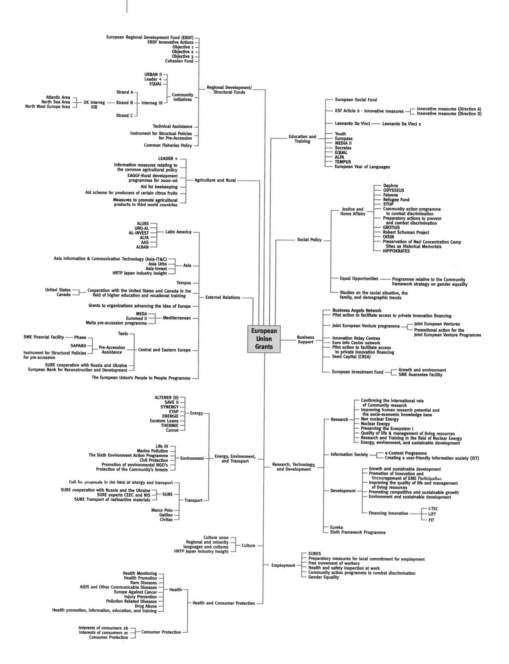

Government

At the upper end of UK government funding are the Framework bids that (say the DTI) can take three person-months to write. Clearly, individuals must tailor the time spent on the bidding process to the likelihood of success. Sometimes there are staged bids, where those short-listed are invited to flesh out the detail (of course, with no guarantees of success).

Government departments

The main government departments offering grant schemes at all levels are:

Department for Education and Skills

<http://www.dfes.gov.uk/>

Department of Health

<http://www.doh.gov.uk/sect64/grants.htm>

Department for Transport

<http://www.dft.gov.uk/>

Department of Trade and Industry

<http://www.dti.gov.uk/>

Countryside Agency

<http://www.countryside.gov.uk/>

Home Office

<http://www.homeoffice.gov.uk/>

Department of Culture, Media and Sport

<http://www.culture.gov.uk/>

Department for Environment, Food and Rural Affairs

<http://www.defra.gov.uk/>

Major funding bodies

Did you know?
In the UK there are over 3,500 different grants offering more than £50 billion.

As a guide . . .
the Department of Health awarded 599 grants to some 394 different organizations in 2002–2003 totalling £22 million.

Tip
There are local offices for:
- the North East
- the North West
- Yorkshire and the Humber
- the West Midlands
- the East Midlands
- the East of England
- the South West
- the South East
- London
- Scotland
- Wales
- Ireland

Department for Work and Pensions

<http://www.dwp.gov.uk/index.htm>

Urban policy unit

<http://www.urban.odpm.gov.uk/>

Community development foundation

<http://www.cdf.org.uk/html/menu.html>

Neighbourhood Renewal Unit

(e.g. Single Regeneration Budget partnerships (SRBs), Local Strategic Partnerships, Health Action Zones (HAZs), Education Action Zones (EAZs), Education Business Partnerships (EBPs), and others).

<http://www.neighbourhood.gov.uk/>

Local Council

Try your local authority as it probably has officers who liaise with the voluntary sector. It may have community development officers who can help with funding ideas for voluntary and community groups.

Charities

The Association of Charitable Foundations exists to promote good practice among trusts and foundations and to educate the public about them. This is a shortened version of its advice.

There are about 8,800 independent grant-making trusts and foundations in the UK. Most UK foundations give grants and nothing else. (The title 'trust' is often used instead of 'foundation', and other titles such as 'settlement' or 'fund' are common. There are some legal differences between these terms that need not concern us here.)

Trusts and foundations vary enormously. Some donate internationally, some nationally, and some give only in a local area. A trust or foundation may be able to give funds for any charitable purpose, or be restricted to a particular subject (e.g. the arts) or to a particular beneficiary group (e.g. children). The larger foundations give tens of millions of pounds (Euros) or more each year, while the smaller ones give only a few thousand. A board of trustees controls every foundation/trust.

UK trusts and foundations give about £2 billion (Euro 3.1 billion) in grants each year to charities (which include universities and religious organizations). About 64% of trusts and foundations give in the health and social welfare fields, 28% give to the arts and recreation (largely sport), and 8% give to causes related to religion.

Trusts and foundations like to donate in areas that the government does not fund. For example:

- new methods of tackling problems;
- disadvantaged and minority groups which have trouble using ordinary services, or which are inadequately served by them;
- responses to new or newly-discovered needs and problems;
- work which is hard to finance through conventional fund-raising;
- one-off purchases or projects;
- short and medium-term work which is likely to bring a long-term benefit and/or to attract long-term funding from elsewhere.

Most trusts and foundations derive their income from an endowment, i.e. a capital sum given to them by a rich individual, family, or organization. It provides a tax-exempt income which funds the grant-giving.

Grant-making trusts and foundations are regulated under the same laws as other UK charities. In England and Wales, they must be registered with the Charity Commission, a semi-independent government body. 182,000 charities are presently registered, with a total income of £24 billion (Euro 38 billion). Grant-making trusts and foundations are a small proportion of the total—6% numerically, and 8% by income. Trusts and foundations are thus required to be transparent about their work.

Major funding bodies

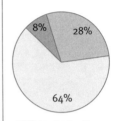

- Health/welfare
- Arts/recreation
- Religion

Major industries which sponsor UK events:

- Insurance
- Alcohol
- Banks
- Motors
- Sports goods/ clothing
- Grocery
- Media
- Power generation
- Non-alcoholic drinks

Agency addresses

NB The details below were correct as of February 2003 and may change.

Action with Communities in Rural England (ACRE)
Supports rural community development.
Somerford Court
Somerford Road
Cirencester GL7 1TW
tel: 01285 653477
<http://www.acre.org.uk/>

Arts Council of England
Supports and develops the arts in England. Much funding of the arts in England is done by Regional Arts Boards.
14 Great Peter Street
London SW1P 3NQ
tel: 020 7333 0100
<http://www.artscouncil.org.uk/>

Association of Charitable Foundations
Promotes larger grant-making charitable trusts and foundations.
2 Plough Yard
Shoreditch High Street
London EC2A 3LP
tel: 020 7422 8600
<http://www.acf.org.uk/>

Arts Council of Northern Ireland
Receives and distributes arts money (including arts lottery money) in Northern Ireland.
Macneice House
77 Malone Road
Belfast BT9 6AQ
tel: 028 90 385200
<http://www.artscouncil-ni.org/>

Arts Council of Wales
Receives and distributes arts money (including arts lottery money) in Wales.
Holst House
9 Museum Place
Cardiff CF1 3NX
<http://www.artswales.org.uk/>

Arts and Business
Formerly called the Association for Business Sponsorship in the Arts (ABSA). Encourages the private sector to support the arts. See bibliography for details of its periodically-updated Sponsorship Manual.
Head Office (there are regional offices)
Nutmeg House
60 Gainsford Street
London SE1 2NY
tel: 020 7407 7525
<http://www.aandb.org.uk/>

Business in the Community
Encourages companies to get involved in schemes which contribute to social and economic regeneration. Covers England, Wales, and Northern Ireland.
137 Shepherdess Walk
London N1 7RQ
tel: 0870 600 2482
<http://www.bitc.org.uk/>

Charities Aid Foundation
A large national charity that provides all sorts of services to charitable donors, does research into things charitable, and publishes a wide range of books and directories. See page 130 for details of its Directory of Grant-Making Trusts, published every two years.
Kings Hill
West Malling
Kent ME19 4TA
tel: 01732 520 000
<http://www.cafonline.org/>

City Action
Broker between City firms and community-based organizations.
28 Park Street
London SE1 9EO
tel: 020 7236 2996
<http://www.city-action.org/>

Community Development Foundation
A community-based charity.
60 Highbury Grove
London N5 2AG
tel: 020 7226 5375
<http://www.cdf.org.uk/>

Charity Commission for England and Wales
Part of government that (in England and Wales) registers and
regulates charities. Has some free publications.
Harmsworth House
13–15 Bouverie Street
London EC4Y 8DP
tel: 0870 333 0123
<http://www.charity-commission.gov.uk/>

Federation of Rural Community Councils
William House
Shipton Road
Skelton, York YO3 6XW
tel: 01904 645271

The Heart of the City
Helps companies in the City and Docklands to become more
involved in community and charity work.
PO Box 270, Guildhall
London EC2P 2EJ
tel: 020 7332 3643
<http://www.theheartofthecity.com/>

Institute of Sports Sponsorship
Promotes best practice in sponsorship; works closely with sports
bodies, government, and the media.
Warwick House
25–27 Buckingham Palace Road
London SW1W 0PP
tel: 020 7233 7747
<http://www.sports-sponsorship.co.uk/>

National Association of Councils for Voluntary Service (England)
Arundel Court
177 Arundel Street
Sheffield S1 2NU
tel: 0114 278 6636
<http://www.nacvs.org.uk/>

National Council for Voluntary Organisations (England)
Regents Wharf, 8 All Saints Street
London N1 9RL
tel: 020 7713 6161
<http://ncvo-vol.org.uk/>

National Endowment for Science, Technology and the Arts (NESTA)
Supports talent, innovation, and creativity in science, technology,
and the arts across the UK. NESTA mainly gives grants to individuals.
Fishmongers' Chambers
110 Upper Thames Street
London EC4R 3TJ
tel: 020 7645 9500
<http://www.nesta.org.uk/>

Regional Arts Boards
Independent organizations that develop and fund arts activities in
the regions. They also distribute some of the arts lottery funding.
<http://www.arts.org.uk/>

Scottish Arts Council
Develops arts activities in Scotland.
12 Manor Place
Edinburgh EH3 7DD
tel: 0131 226 6051
<http://www.sac.org.uk/>

Scottish Business in the Community
Encourages companies to get involved in schemes which
contribute to social and economic regeneration in Scotland.
PO Box 408, Bankhead Avenue
Edinburgh EH11 4HE
tel: 0131 442 2020
<http://www.sbcscot.com/>

Scottish Council for Voluntary Organisations
Umbrella body for voluntary organizations in Scotland.
The Mansfield, Traquair Centre
15 Mansfield Place
Edinburgh EH3 6BB
tel: 0131 556 3882
<http://www.scvo.org.uk/>

Wales Council for Voluntary Action
13 Wynnstay Road, Colwyn Bay
Conwy LL29 8NB
tel: 01492 539800
<http://www.wcva.org.uk/>

Further reading

Trusts

The following publications give comprehensive information about trusts in the UK and abroad.

A Guide to the Major Trusts, Volumes 1 and/or 2 for UK-wide trusts, priced £19.95 each plus p&p; and Volume 3 for trusts funding in Scotland, Wales, and Northern Ireland, priced £17.95 plus p&p.

Directory of Grant Making Trusts, £75.00 plus p&p.

The International Development Directory, £16.95 plus p&p. Information about trusts which give in the developing world, and about UK-based international charities.

Dimensions of the Voluntary Sector (3 volumes), £32.50 plus p&p, published by Charities Aid Foundation.

The above are available from the Directory of Social Change, 24 Stephenson Way, London NW1 2DP, tel: 020 7209 5151, <http://www.dsc.org.uk/>.

City of London Directory and Livery Companies Guide, £24 incl. p&p. City Press, Sea Trade House, 42 North Station Road, Colchester, CO1 1RB, tel: 01206 545121.

Useful One Step Ahead titles

Editing and Revising Text by Jo Billingham (OUP, 2002)

Giving Presentations by Jo Billingham (OUP, 2003)

Presenting Numbers, Tables, and Charts by Sally Bigwood and Melissa Spore (OUP, 2003)

Writing Reports by John Seely (OUP, 2002)

Bibliography

I have consulted the following books and gained ideas from them.

Arts & Business Sponsorship Manual (Fourth edition), £15, Arts & Business; ISBN 00951240986 (2001).
Details five steps for obtaining arts sponsorship in the UK. Very useful advice and listing of arts funding contact addresses.

Director's Briefing Notes: Writing a Business Plan, Business Hotline Publications; ISBN 13691996 (2001).

Hollis Sponsorship and Donations Yearbook, £115, Hollis Publications Ltd.; ISBN 090096703X (published annually in January).

How to Write Proposals and Reports That Get Results
Ros Jay, £9.99, Financial Times Prentice Hall; ISBN 0273644971 (1999).
A step-by-step guide to writing a report or proposal from start to finish. The text covers structure, grammar, and presentation, with exercises. This book gave me the idea for the five 'P's.

How to Write Successful Fund-raising Letters
Mal Warwick, £20.95, Jossey-Bass; ISBN 078795652X (2001).
Moderately useful to a UK readership, because it is very US-focused.

Persuasive Reports and Proposals
Andrew Leigh, £5.95, Chartered Institute of Personnel and Development (CIPD); ISBN 0852928092 (1999).
A short and succinct book with a few useful exercises.

About the author

At various points, this book has stressed the importance of establishing your credentials. A sense of who you are (or whom you represent) gives your prospective employer, client, or funder reasons why they should trust you.

So let me do that for you now. As a freelancer for over 30 years, I have had plenty of experience of writing proposals—ideas for books, articles, consultancy jobs, and many others. For seven years I was part of a team that was constantly putting out tenders for partnerships between education and industry. This involved co-ordinating and editing other people's bids for substantial company and government funding. Knocking other people's prose into shape taught me a great deal about the need for clear objectives and helpful sign-posting. I almost always had to read and re-read my colleagues' work searching for the main point; expressing it succinctly; and moving it to the top.

I am also on a judging committee that meets twice a year to assess private grants proposals. And, as a board director, I have frequently been part of an assessment team reviewing a shortlist of bids for work for a company. So I have been at the other end of seeing how people put themselves across; what works and what does not. I have also seen how arbitrary, sometimes, an acceptance or rejection is. Making the most of your positive assets really does count as it can be the smallest detail that sways an application one way or the other.

These activities have shown me that most people are so close to their particular cause that they do not sufficiently think about how it comes across to someone outside it. It is the intention of this book to help readers widen their horizons.

Index